MW00934429

Hermeticism

The Ultimate Guide to Understanding the Hermetica, Kybalion, and Hermetic Principles

© Copyright 2021

The contents of this book may not be reproduced, duplicated or transmitted without direct written permission from the author.

Under no circumstances will any legal responsibility or blame be held against the publisher for any reparation, damages, or monetary loss due to the information herein, either directly or indirectly.

Legal Notice:

This book is copyright protected. This is only for personal use. You cannot amend, distribute, sell, use, quote or paraphrase any part or the content within this book without the consent of the author.

Disclaimer Notice:

Please note the information contained within this document is for educational and entertainment purposes only. Every attempt has been made to provide accurate, up to date and reliable complete information. No warranties of any kind are expressed or implied. Readers acknowledge that the author is not engaging in the rendering of legal, financial, medical or professional advice. The content of this book has been derived from various sources. Please consult a licensed professional before attempting any techniques outlined in this book.

By reading this document, the reader agrees that under no circumstances is the author responsible for any losses, direct or indirect, which are incurred as a result of the use of information contained within this document, including, but not limited to, —errors, omissions, or inaccuracies.

Your Free Gift (only available for a limited time)

Thanks for getting this book! If you want to learn more about various spirituality topics, then join Mari Silva's community and get a free guided meditation MP3 for awakening your third eye. This guided meditation mp3 is designed to open and strengthen ones third eye so you can experience a higher state of consciousness. Simply visit the link below the image to get started.

https://spiritualityspot.com/meditation

Contents

Introduction

Hermeticism is a philosophy rooted in ancient Egypt and Greece. The doctrines of Hermeticism have been passed on by word of mouth, and today, this belief system exists through *The Kybalion*, a book written by the "Three Initiates" whose real identities are unknown.

The secrets revealed in Hermeticism have the power to change your way of thinking so much that your life could transform into something magical. You need to read this book to understand more about it.

This book holds the essentials of Hermeticism written in simple language that everyone can understand, including detailed descriptions of the principles, instructions, and hands-on methods. It is like a one-shop-stop for beginners.

All elements about this esoteric philosophy are covered in the following pages, from the origins of this ancient philosophical system right up to its present-day practical implications and applications. You will not have to refer to any other source unless you want to delve deeper than beginner level. It includes up-to-date information and is engaging enough that you can complete the first reading in one stretch and have a good understanding of the topic.

When you have finished your first reading, you can then return to it chapter by chapter and follow the instructions given in each to implement the hermetic way of living and thinking into your life. As you savor the outcomes of each method and thought process described, you will realize the effects of adhering to the magical principles of Hermeticism in your life as it gets more fulfilling and meaningful.

In addition to dedicated chapters for each of the principles, you will get an overall idea of how to put into practice the theoretical teachings of Hermeticism. Reading this book will not be relegated to mere theory; you can apply the theory to your practical life and positively transform yourself and the world around you.

The hermetic student in you is calling you to keep reading. It is a sure-shot way to begin the enchanting journey of Hermeticism, and you will undoubtedly fuel yourself to move forward until you master the wonderful philosophy.

So, go on, turn the page, read on, and be amazed . . .

Chapter 1: Hermes Trismegistus and the Kybalion

The first question to find answers to before delving into the principles and belief systems of Hermeticism is "Who was/is Hermes Trismegistus?"

As a brief introduction, Hermes Trismegistus (or Hermes T) is central to Hermeticism, Hermetic principles, and the Kybalion. The Jewish tradition claims that Hermes T was a contemporary of the revered Jewish patriarch, Abraham, which means Hermeticism originated over 5,000 years ago.

Additionally, he was referred to as the scribe of the gods by ancient Egyptians, as the god of wisdom by the ancient Greeks, as Mercury by the ancient Romans, etc. He discovered alchemy and astrology and is considered the original source from which all Hermeticism flows.

Hermes Trismegistus

Hermes Trismegistus is believed to have authored the *Corpus Hermeticum*, the sacred texts of Hermeticism. Hermes Trismegistus means "thrice-born Hermes." He is associated with the Greek God Hermes and the Egyptian god Thoth. Both Hermes and Thoth are believed to be the messengers of the gods. In Egypt, Thoth and Hermes are worshipped as One. In fact, the Temple of Thoth in Khemenu was called Hermopolis during the Greek period.

Hermes was the god of communication and messages. He was believed to carry messages between human beings and the gods. He is also known to help human beings interpret messages from the gods. In Egypt, Thoth is also worshipped as the god of wisdom. Some people believe that Imhotep, the ancient Egyptian polymath and priest, was Thoth. Other humans and divine beings who were treated as being equal to Thoth were:

- Teos, a wise man in Egyptian mythology.

- Amenhotep, the famous Egyptian scribe.

Both these people had their shrines within the temples of Thoth and Hermes. Other mythological figures whom Hermes is associated with include:

- Mercury — Mercury was the Roman equivalent of Hermes as he was considered the messenger of gods and the god of commerce.

- Enoch — Enoch appeared in the Bible and was the great-grandfather of Noah. Enoch ascends to Heaven and becomes an archangel called Metraton. He also becomes the scribe of the gods.

- Idris — Islamic equivalent of Enoch.

Marcus Tullius Cicero, a Roman scholar and statesman, lists many references that connect Hermes and Thoth. Two important references are:

- Hermes was the son of the River Nile.

- Hermes killed Argus Panoptes, the multi-eyed giant in Greek mythology. He then had to escape to Egypt. There he was addressed as "Theyt." According to Cicero, this Hermes who fled to Egypt after killing the monster taught the Egyptians their alphabets and law.

These references of Cicero are what most experts draw on to accept that Hermes Trismegistus had his origins in Greek-controlled Egypt, thanks to the syncretism between the Egyptian and Greek gods. Hermes Trismegistus is credited with having written thousands of texts and scriptures, nearly all held in high esteem and reputed to be of great antiquity.

For example, Seleucus I Nicator, a Greek general of Alexander the Great, accounts for 20,000 works that he credits to Hermes T, and Manetho, an Egyptian priest who is believed to have lived in the third century BCE., credits over 36,000 texts and writings to Hermes. From all these writings, about 42 of them were kept in the Great Library of Alexandria.

Clement of Alexandria, the famous Christian theologian and philosopher, believed that there are 42 Egyptian sacred writings credited to Hermes, which could be the ones that were preserved in the library of Alexandria. These writings detailed the training of Egyptian priests. *The Hermetica* is a specific collection of papyri or ancient writings containing spells and other initiatory induction procedures for Egyptian priests.

It also describes the spells needed to capture the souls of angels and demons and capture them in statues so that the statue could speak and foretell the future. Other ancient documents contain recipes using herbs, odors, and gems to trap these souls, along with descriptions of how to create and animate the idols.

Many Christian writers of the Middle Ages, including Augustine, Lactantius, Marsilio Ficino, Campanella, and others, considered Hermes Trismegistus to be a wise pagan sage or prophet who believed in the coming of Christianity. The *Corpus Hermeticum* contains references to:

- The Son of God.

- A creation story similar to the Biblical one.

- The Creative word.

Lactantius, who lived in the third and fourth centuries, says that Hermes T was a man of great antiquity and immense wisdom and knowledge. According to Lactantius, Hermes asserted the existence and importance of only one God and called Him as God and Father, similar to Christians.

The coming of Christianity was given to humans in ancient times, according to Medieval Age Christian writers. The earlier prophets who prophesied the origin and growth of Christianity included Zoroaster and Plato. Christianity adopted Hermetic teachings and considered Hermes Trismegistus to be either a contemporary of Moses or the third in line of wise Egyptians, namely Enoch, Noah, and Hermes, the priest-king of Egypt.

Hermes is referred to as Trismegistus because of statements mentioned in the Emerald Tablet of Hermes Trismegistus, where he is believed to know the three parts of the wisdom of the universe, including:

- Alchemy — the operation of the Sun.

- Astrology — the operation of the stars. Hermes credits Zoroaster, the Zoroastrian religion founder (who lived in 2 BCE), with creating astrology.

- Theurgy — the operation of the gods.

In another reference in Suda, the famous Byzantine Encyclopedia, he is known as the Thrice-Great because of his praise for the Trinity and saying that there is only one divine nature even in the Trinity.

So, it is clear that Hermes T is not considered just one individual. Instead, he is believed to be a combination of many distinctive mythological figures—though scholars believe that he was a real wise sage who lived thousands of years ago. The interesting point to note here is that for the followers of Hermeticism, the real identity of Hermes is inconsequential. They focus on the Hermetic teachings and try to adhere to the principles in their daily life.

Works and Beliefs of Hermes Trismegistus

All the texts written by Hermes were allegedly received through divine wisdom when he was in meditative trances. He is believed to have covered numerous topics, including chemistry, medicine, art, law, magic, music, philosophy, geography, anatomy, and mathematics. His knowledge was so extensive that the Egyptians referred to him as the gods' communicator or messenger.

Hermes Trismegistus's writings are collectively known as *The Hermetica*, of which the most important surviving works include *The Asclepius* and the *Corpus Hermeticum*. Until the Renaissance period, it was generally accepted that Hermes Trismegistus was Moses's contemporary.

Isaac Casaubon, a classical philologist and one of the most scholarly men of his time in Europe, dated Hermetic writings no earlier than the second or third century CE. According to Yates Giordano Bruno, in his study of Hermetic Tradition, *The Hermetica* was written by multiple unknown authors, mostly of Greek origin. The contents are primarily Hellenistic in outlook combining Stoicism Platonism, a smattering of Jewish teachings, and a bit of Persian influence.

References to Platonism in the *Hermeticum Corpus* include the following elements:

- A creation story similar to the one that Plato describes in his *Timaeus.*

- A tripartite hierarchy.

- References to the dual nature of human beings.

During the Medieval Ages and the Renaissance Period, the elements of Hermeticism were popular among alchemists. Typically, the Hermetic Traditions refers to three subjects, namely Alchemy, Astrology, and Theurgy. The Hermetic writings were broadly divided into two primary categories: technical Hermetica and philosophical Hermetica.

The technical Hermetica deals with alchemy, magic, and magic potions; philosophical Hermetica deals with philosophy.

Interestingly, the term "Hermetically sealed" originates from the procedure given in *The Hermetica* to make the Philosopher's Stone a legendary alchemical substance. According to the procedure, the required mixture of raw materials was placed in a glass vessel, and the neck of this vessel is fused using another process called the Seal of Hermes.

There is an Islamic connection to Hermes Trismegistus. According to Sayyid Ahmed Amiruddin, a Canadian who worked diligently on a systemized practice to prevent radicalization, early Islamic and Christian traditions believe that Hermes Trismegistus was the builder of the Pyramids of Giza, an important place in Islamic traditions.

He also says that Hermes Trismegistus is mentioned in the Koran as a prophet and was highly revered for his truthfulness. Another vital Islamic connection to Hermeticism is that the oldest documented source of the Emerald Tablet of Hermes Trismegistus is contained in the Jabirian corpus, and so the Hermetic Tradition and writings were considered sacred in Islam as well.

According to certain Islamic writings, Hermes is believed to be Idris, the prophet who traveled to outer space from Egypt, went to Heaven, and returned to Earth carrying many objects of Adam from Eden. Ancient Arab genealogists believe that Prophet Muhammad is a direct descendant of Hermes Trismegistus.

Within the occult tradition, it is believed that Hermes Trismegistus had several wives and fathered numerous sons, many of whom took his name. His grandchildren also took his name. The repetition of Hermes's name through various generations could account for the longevity of the revered individual. This approach is even more believable if you consider that many of his future generations also took up the priesthood's occupation in several mysterious and mystical religions and belief systems.

What is Hermeticism?

Hermeticism combines Science, Philosophy, and Metaphysics. As already explained, the three essential aspects of Hermeticism are Astrology, Alchemy, and Theurgy. Interestingly, Alchemy is a tradition that goes back millennia, and it has influenced the origin and development of modern medicine, chemistry, psychology, and philosophy. Western alchemy is an important branch of Hermetic philosophy.

Hermeticism is one of the oldest traditions blending philosophical and religious tenets and thoughts. It flourished in Ptolemaic Egypt, which lasted from 305 BCE to 30 BCE. The belief system was not represented by any single religious group but formed the foundation and root of many traditions.

The word "hermetic" refers to being protected or sealed, which refers to "being kept secret." "Concealing" tenets of Hermeticism and driving Hermetic followers underground was the need of the hour during the Medieval Ages, thanks to high levels of persecution. History gives proof of how hermetics were ostracized, burned at the stake, and tormented by the powers of those times.

Hermeticism and Hermetic philosophy has always been seen as "occult." This word has nothing to do with religion or black magic. It simply implied "kept hidden."

Hermeticism combines ancient Egyptian philosophy, religion, magic, and science along with influences from ancient religions of the Sumerian Civilization, Platonism, Alexandrian Judaism, Greek Paganism, Zoroastrianism, and more. Hermeticism is believed to hold the "Prisca theologia." This ancient doctrine claims to be the root of all global religions and was given to human beings in antiquity.

Hermeticism believes in the existence of one transcendent God and that "All is One" in the universe, as well as multiple other cosmic beings such as elementals, eons, and angels. Scholars believe Hermeticism influenced major religions, such as Judaism, Christianity, and Islam.

Hermeticism and the Scientific Revolution

Hermeticism influenced many scientists right from ancient times. Some of them include:

• Pythagoras — This ancient Greek mathematician is believed to have been an initiate in the Hermetic arts after studying them in Egypt.

• Plato — Pythagoras deeply influenced Plato, who was inspired by Hermetic teachings. There are several claims that Plato learned about Hermeticism from Egyptian teachers.

• Aristotle — Aristotle was Plato's pupil and Alexander the Great's teacher. The Greek emperor conquered Egypt in 343 BCE and laid the foundation stone of Alexandria, one of the most important learning centers for Hermeticism and alchemy.

Hermeticism, Neoplatonism, and natural magic influenced the Scientific Revolution's growth and development during the Renaissance period. Although the Scientific Revolution embraced open inquiry, logical reasoning, and empiricism, the Renaissance period witnessed a resurgence of Hermetic metaphorical, magical, and mythical ideas and thought processes.

It must be remembered that the founders of modern science were deeply religious people, and many of them were esotericists and alchemists, both of which had deep roots in Hermeticism. Copernicus quotes Hermes when he describes the Sun in his heliocentric model of the cosmos. Isaac Newton practiced alchemy, which influenced many of his modern scientific discoveries.

One of the most significant changes during the Scientific Revolution and the Renaissance period was the separation of science and religion and the spiritual realm. Until the middle of the seventeenth century, natural philosophy saw nature as a dynamic, organic, living, interconnected organism. There was no separation between astrology and astronomy, alchemy and chemistry, or science and magic. These elements were differentiated as separate entities and categorized either as science or religion.

In science, the observed phenomenon is distinguished from the observer and their perceptions, internal value, and belief systems. When science witnesses a phenomenon, it assumes that what is happening in the nature of the phenomenon and what the observer sees is reality. Thanks to many advancements made in quantum and relativity theories of science, it was seen that the object under observation could behave differently when the observational process and/or the observer changes or is eliminated from the equation.

In Hermeticism, the observer, their nature and reflections, and the observed phenomenon or object are intrinsically linked. According to Hermetic philosophy, the outside universe reflects your thoughts, ideas, perceptions, and whatever is happening inside you. The goal of seeking knowledge is to reunite with the universal divine or the "Great Work" of humankind. Hermeticism's core belief is embedded in the famous phrase, "As above, so below."

Much of the ancient Hermetic wisdom coded in various literature and alchemy texts were destroyed around the third and fourth centuries. Whatever was left was transferred to the Islamic world and revived only during the Renaissance. Thanks to persecution by those in power in those times, many practicing Hermetics were forced to go underground, Hermeticism an "occultist" shade.

Many of the Hermetic ideas permeated into Western esoteric traditions, including these secret societies:

- Freemasons
- Rosicrucians
- The Hermetic Order of the Golden Dawn
- Thelema
- Modern Paganism
- Wicca

The Kybalion

Modern occultists believe that Hermetic writings could be of Pharaonic origin. The 42 essential texts spoken about by Clement of Alexandria contain Hermeticism's core religious beliefs, and these texts are not available in the public domain. In its place is *The Kybalion*, the sacred book written by The Three Initiates containing and addressing Hermetic beliefs and principles.

Historically, the teachings of Hermeticism were passed on orally. For the first time, the Three Initiates decided to write them down so that a wider audience could have access to Hermetic ideas and thoughts. The Three Initiates, to whom the creation of *The Kybalion* is credited, are not named anywhere. Many followers believe and/or suspect the three of them to be Yogi Ramacharaka, Baba Bharata, and William Walker Atkinson.

It was first published in 1908 by the Yogi Publication Society. It is revered as a sacred and vital tool needed to understand the spiritual and physical planes separately and integrate an understanding of these two planes.

The Kybalion is a collection of Hermetic teachings and ideas based on the principles and morals as explained and described by Hermes Trismegistus. It is considered to help students of Hermeticism unlock the fundamentals of esoteric philosophy. Seven basic principles that apply to everything in the cosmos form the basis of Hermeticism in *The Kybalion.*

Students of comparative religions all over the world see doctrines of Hermeticism in every faith. The idea that Hermeticism is the root of all major religions seems to have some truth to it. *The Kybalion* is not only meant for scholars; it can be read, understood, and the tenets implemented by any interested individual.

The basic doctrines explained in this powerful book deal with mastering the mind and the mental forces. It helps you improve and build your mind's power to such an extent that highly experienced practitioners can transmute from one vibrational state to another. Reading, understanding, and implementing *The Kybalion's* principles allows you to change your perception of reality.

This chapter ends with important Hermetic axioms:

- Wisdom is taught only to those who are ready to understand. This vital axiom keeps powerful teachings from those who want to use them to control others. To have understanding is to make sure the teachings are used wisely and for the good of all.

- Those who are ready to learn from the Master will open their ears wide to listen to His teachings.

- Wisdom will come only when a student is ready and prepared to hear and accept.

There are Seven Principles of Truth, and the person who knows and understands these will have the keys to open the doors of the Temple.

The Seven Hermetic Principles include (each of these principles is discussed in detail in separate chapters of this book):

- The Principle of Mentalism — Everything in the mind of all is mental.

- The Principle of Correspondence — The reality you experience is based on your thoughts, or your thoughts reflect the reality you experience.

- The Principle of Vibration — When you feel an emotion or thought, you attract people who feel and think the same way.

- The Principle of Polarity — What you see as opposites are nothing but varying degrees of the same thing.

- The Principle of Rhythm — The pendulum of life is always swinging.

- The Principle of Cause and Effect — All things in the world are driven by cause and effect, and there are no accidents.

- The Principle of Gender — All things in the world have feminine and masculine aspects or energies.

Chapter 2: Hermetic Philosophy Basics: The All, the Elements, and the Seven Universal Laws

Hermeticism is considered the most influential, unified, and all-encompassing spiritual movement started in Western antiquity. It was a cultural and spiritual movement that syncretized ancient Egyptian and Greco-Roman religious and philosophical systems.

Magical practices, cosmologies, and philosophies prevalent in ancient times mingled and mixed to create a distinct and syncretic philosophical and spiritual practice system and thought. Here are the Hermetic threads found in other systems.

The Cosmic Egg — The Cosmic Egg concept exists in Greek mythology and is referred to as the Orphic Egg. According to Greek beliefs, the cosmos came from a silver egg, depicted frequently with a serpent coiled around it.

The Tarot — Most occultists believe that the tarot found its way to Europe from India through Egypt. However, there are suggestions of Egyptian prototype tarot cards, or at least a few concepts originated in Egypt. In such a scenario, the tarot could have originated in Hermetic and Egyptian beliefs.

The Caduceus — Hermes T is often depicted holding the caduceus wand, a classic Greco-Roman symbol. This wand has two serpents coiled around it and also has wings on the top. The snakes are comparable to the Indian system of Kundalini, a form of energy believed to be seated at the base of the spine in the form of a coiled snake.

The All

According to Hermeticism, God is the Infinite Creator's life force or the "All Mind" or simply the "All." This "All" is the source of all three planes and is beyond energy, matter, space, time, and laws because it is the highest force of Creation. The reality and nature of the "All Mind" or God that many people relate to transcends human and earthly understanding.

You can comprehend that this "All" or the source of all creation is everywhere and within everything. It occupies little space in the cosmos, and everyone lives within this omnipresent "All," which is an all-encompassing Divine mind. Each mind is a creation, part, and an extension of this All, or the Divine Mind.

The All is unchangeable as it is the absolute Mind that has always existed, and each of the infinite universes it creates is continuously changing. The Kybalion says that "The All creates countless universes in its Infinite Mind which exist for eons. Yet, for the All, creation, growth, and decline or death of a million universes happens in the twinkling of an eye. According to the Kybalion, *'The 'All Mind' is the infinite mind of the cosmos.'*"

The Elements

The Kybalion has had a great influence on modern Western Mystery Tradition. The Principle of Correspondence in Hermeticism is a primary aspect in many of the western magical belief systems. According to this principle, the physical world is a reflection of the spiritual world and vice versa. Moreover, there is harmony between the two planes and the elements of nature. The four Hermetic elements are fire, earth, air, and water. You will come to understand these four elements in this chapter.

The Greeks are believed to have proposed the existence of the five basic elements, namely fire, air, water, and earth (the four physical elements), and spirit (or Aether or Quintessence), as a more rarified, non-physical element. Interestingly, the word "quintessence" translates to "fifth element" in Latin.

Also, the elements are hierarchical, according to Western occult theory. The order of the elements is spirit, fire, air, water, and earth. The first three elements are spiritual, while the last two elements are materialistic. Before the Renaissance Period, magicians, spiritual seekers, and scientists were aligned with each other and were not at loggerheads. There was much overlap between the discoveries and practices of spirituality (or magic) and science until the Renaissance, with alchemy a bridge between the two disciplines.

One particular polyglot who lived in the Renaissance Period (1574 to 1637) was Robert Fludd. This English alchemist, Qabalist, astrologer, cosmologist, and mathematician, like many other scientists-alchemists of that time, tried to examine and understand the different planes of existence and how they corresponded with one another. People like Robert Fludd also observed the natural world keenly.

For example, they could see that elemental air formed intermediary energy between fire and water and reconciled these two elements in the large universe or the Macrocosm. Interestingly, they also saw that these elements and their functions were reflected in the small universe or the Microcosm, in the physical human body.

These scientists-alchemists realized that the human body could inhale air into the lungs and convert it into energy (fire), which was delivered to all parts of the body through the blood and lymph, which represent water (or liquid). The following section details each of the four physical elements, including their qualities and symbols.

Elemental Qualities

Every element has two qualities, and each of these qualities is shared with another element. Here are the two elemental qualities.

Cold or Warm — Each of the elements is either cold or warm. Interestingly, a dichotomy exists here. Cold qualities such as dark, passive, and receptive are considered to be particular to the feminine gender. Warm qualities like light, activity, and warmth are masculine characteristics. The dichotomy is an interesting angle, considering most people are familiar with these qualities in reverse.

Also, warm male elements are oriented upward in the symbolic triangle and ascend toward the spiritual realm. Cold, female elements are oriented downward and descend into the earth.

Dry or Moist — The second pair of elemental qualities are connected to dryness or moistness, which do not correspond to any other ideas or concepts.

Opposing Elements

Each of the four elements shares one of its two qualities with another element. This means each element is completely unrelated to one of the other three elements; for example, the air is warm like fire and moist like water, so it is unrelated to the earth element.

These opposing elements are on the opposite sides of the traditional elemental diagram, represented by two straight lines intersecting each other at right angles, resulting in four equal quadrants. Moreover, each element is represented by a triangle, two of them with crossbars and two without.

Fire and water are opposing elements and do not have crossbars in their triangles. Air and earth are also opposites, and the triangles of these two elements have crossbars on them.

Elemental Hierarchy, Elemental Pentagram, and Other Correspondences

Traditionalists place the elements in a hierarchical system where the lower elements are physical and materialistic, while the higher elements are more rarefied, less physical, and more spiritual. The four elements are in the following elemental hierarchy:

Earth is the lowest and the most materialistic element.

Moving clockwise from the earth is water.

Air comes next, and the fire is the least materialistic element.

The pentagram has multiple symbolic meanings in various cultures and traditions since ancient times. From the Renaissance Period, the pentagram is associated with the four elements and the fifth, namely the spirit. Here are how the five elements are represented through a pentagram.

As already explained, the elements are placed in a hierarchical system ranging from the most spiritual and least materialistic to the least spiritual and most materialistic. This order is the determining factor in the arrangement of the elements around the pentagram.

To trace an elemental pentagram, you need to start with the spirit, which is the highest element. The fire element is on the lower right side of the spirit element. Air is at the upward left point from fire, just below the spirit. The water element is the opposite of air and is connected with a horizontal line. Earth is at the low left point of water. The last line connecting the earth and spirit completes the pentagram.

The symbolic meaning of the pentagram changes with its orientation. If the pentagram is pointed upward, the spirit is at the top. This means that the spirit rules over all the other elements. When the pentagram is pointed downward, the spirit is right at the bottom. This means the spirit element has descended into all the matter. The colors associated with each element are:

- Spirit — white
- Fire — red
- Air — yellow
- Water — blue
- Earth — green

Nearly all traditional systems connect the four elements with various things of human life, including the four phases of the moon, the four seasons, the four cardinal directions, and the time of the day.

- Earth is associated with North, the new moon, winter, and midnight.

- Air is associated with East, the waxing moon, spring, and sunrise.

- Fire is associated with South, the full moon, summer, and noon.

- Water is associated with West, the waning moon, autumn, and sunset.

Many of the symbolism and teachings of modern Hermeticism are credited to the Hermetic Order of the Golden Dawn, which flourished in the nineteenth century and the early parts of the twentieth century. This highly influential society is often referred to as simply the Golden Dawn. Its members were active participants in the practice and study of theurgy, occultism, paranormal activities, and metaphysics.

Like ancient traditional systems, Hermeticism uses daily, monthly, and annual natural cycles to relate to the periods of growth, decline, fullness, and barrenness of multiple elements experienced by human beings. For example, fire is associated with life and fullness. Fire is often synonymous with the sun and light, so noon, summer, and the full moon are associated with the fire element.

Earth corresponds to midnight, the new moon, and winter. Winter does not necessarily mean death. Rather, the cold, seemingly barren winter is connected with the hidden potential and transformation period after which new life replaces the old. The concept of barrenness in winter is associated with the preparation of the earth to sprout new life in spring.

Air, the element of new beginnings, is associated with spring, sunrise, and the waxing moon. Air is also connected to creativity, youth, and abundance. Things are bright and warm during spring, and animals, plants, and other forms of life give birth to new generations.

Water is associated with wisdom, especially the wisdom that comes with age and experience. Water represents a period that is past the peak of life and moving toward the end of the cycle. The summary of the various symbols for each element is given below.

Fire

Fire stands for activity, strength, life force, and blood. It is considered a purifier and protector. It can consume all impurities and can get rid of darkness. Fire is the most spiritual and rarefied physical element because it does not have a physical existence, has transformative powers, and produces light.

Fire is warm, dry, masculine, and associated with the salamander, a mythical creature that could burst into flames. Its directional association is with the south, and its color is red. The magical tools connected with the fire element are an athame, a sword, a dagger, and a wand. The fire element's planets are the Sun (in many occult systems including Hermeticism, the Sun and Moon are considered planets) and Mars.

The zodiac signs associated with fire are Aries, Leo, and Sagittarius. Its season is summer, and the time of the day is noon.

Air

Air stands for creativity, intelligence, and new beginnings, but it is not entirely tangible and has no permanent form or shape. It's masculine, active, and comes above water and earth in the elemental hierarchy.

Air is warm, moist, and associated with invisible beings called sylphs. Its direction is east, and the color is yellow. The magical tools associated with air are a wand, sword, and dagger.

The planet associated with the air element is Jupiter, while the zodiac signs are Gemini, Libra, and Aquarius. Its season is spring, and the time of day is sunrise or dawn.

Water

Water stands for the unconscious mind and emotions. Water, like earth, has a physical existence and is tangible. It can trigger all five senses in the body. However, it is considered less material and more spiritual and superior to the earth element. It has more movement and activity than earth.

Water is cold, moist, and a feminine element, which means it is passive. The elemental beings that water is associated with are undines or water-based nymphs. Its direction is west, its color is blue, and its season is autumn or fall. The cup is its magical tool. The Moon and Venus are the planets associated with water.

The zodiac signs of water are Cancer, Scorpio, and Pisces. The time of day associated with water is sunset.

Earth

Earth stands for fertility, groundedness, stability, materialism, stillness, and potential. It can also be an element of death and new life. It is often seen as the element of death and rebirth because life comes from the ground and returns to it after death.

Earth is cold, dry, and a feminine element (so it is considered passive). It's associated with gnomes. Earth's direction is north, its color is green, and its magical tool is the pentacle. Earth is associated with the planet Saturn. The zodiac signs are Taurus, Virgo, and Capricorn. Its season is winter, and the time of day is midnight.

Spirit — The Fifth Element

The Spirit element does not have standard correspondences with any physical elements like the other four. It is not physical. The spirit element is known by many names, including aether and quintessence. Although there are no standard symbols associated with the spiritual element, circles are commonly used to represent it. Sometimes spirals and eight-spoked wheels are also used.

In the macrocosm, the spirit element acts as a bridge to connect the physical and spiritual realms. In the microcosm, the spirit bridges the body and soul. According to the Golden Dawn, the direction of the spirit is above, below, and within. The colors associated with the spiritual element are violet, orange, and white.

A widely accepted Hermetic maxim is "dilute and rarify." This brief tenet holds a world of wisdom in it. Hermetic philosophy advises to encourage and condense higher virtues while dissolving your baser behaviors and vices through this maxim. According to Hermeticism, universal and elemental energies are collected in bodies while opposing influences should be expelled.

The elemental properties, such as cold/warm, dry/moist, movement/stillness, and thinness/thickness, are also fundamental properties of existence. The four elements are spiritual analogies to existence. This comparison can also be seen in tarot philosophy and other numerological perspectives. For example, in the fourth card, the Emperor sits on a cube. A cube is four-squared in three-dimensional geometry. It is the symbol of lawfulness and stability in the matter. The Emperor card symbolizes Hermeticism's core, which is the wisdom of lawfulness of the cosmos' existence.

The Planes of Existence and How They Are Interconnected

According to Hermeticism, three planes of existence exist, namely the spiritual, mental, and physical planes. Hermetic philosophy believes that a deep connection exists between these planes, as they continually influence each other. This belief of continuous and harmonious interconnection and interdependence among the three places follows the Law of Attraction.

The Law of Attraction states that your thoughts (mental plane) can affect the world around you (the physical plane.) Similarly, your spiritual and emotional aspects influence the way your life pans out. The planes of existence are also related to each other's frequency. Your physical world automatically shifts its vibration to align with the frequency of your mind (the mental plane). In turn, the vibration of your mental plane is influenced by the vibration of your spiritual plane.

Working on and improving your spiritual vibration will positively affect your mental and physical planes automatically.

The Seven Laws of the Universe — Kybalion

In the last chapter, you just glimpsed the universe's seven principles as promulgated in the Kybalion. Now it is time to dig a little deeper into these seven laws before discussing them in greater detail.

The Principle of Mentalism — The first principle of Hermeticism says, "The All is Mind, and the Cosmos is Mental." Everything that you experience outside and within you is in the mind. This first principle requires the novice Hermetic to take the largest leap of faith.

Quantum level studies demonstrate that particle characteristics and behavior change by the way you choose to measure them. Although this aspect is still not accepted in the scientific world as changes are based on the person/measuring system's expectations, the changes remain a mystery to modern science. Such quantum level studies show that all your experiences and sensations could be entirely based on the thinking of your mind, which is what the Hermetic Principle of Mentalism is all about.

The Principle of Correspondence — According to The Kybalion, "As above, so below. As below, so above." This second principle of Hermeticism states a correspondence between occurrences and laws of the various planes in the cosmos. There is a similarity between big (macrocosm) and small (microcosm) events across the spiritual, mental, and physical planes of existence.

For example, similarities exist between light distribution across the cosmos (macrocosm) and the distribution of neurons in the human brain (microcosm). The behavior of an organization, country, or the world (macrocosm) can also be similar to the behavior of an individual human being (microcosm).

The Principle of Vibration — According to Hermeticism, "Everything is continuously moving and vibrating, nothing is at rest." The constant motion is across all levels of existence, in big and small events in the spiritual, physical, and mental planes.

Modern science talks about this kind of vibration in "string theory," a theoretical model on which scientists hope to model the most fundamental "substance" of the cosmos. These "strings" vibrate in different ways and different dimensions, and depending on the quality and speed of vibration, they can be seen as light, matter, or gravity. This is the same as the Principle of Vibration in Hermeticism.

The Principle of Polarity — The Kybalion says that everything in the universe is dual or has polarity. Everything has its opposite pair. Opposites are identical to each other and differ only in degrees, with the extremes meeting each other. All truths are only half-truths, and all paradoxes are reconcilable.

When air is stretched and compressed at a specific frequency on a physical level, the sound is generated. The polarity here is between the stretched and compressed air. Moods also have polarity between depression and happiness, hate and love, hope and despair, and more at a mental level. Other examples of polarity that you can see all around you include day and night, yin and yang, high and low, black and white, positive and negative, etc.

The Principle of Rhythm — The fifth principle of Hermeticism says that everything rises and falls; it goes in and out, the swing of a pendulum is seen in everything in this cosmos. The swing's measure to the left is the same as the swing's measure to the right. The left and right swings compensate for each other, and this is the rhythm of the universe.

The rhythm of a drum defines the music. The rhythm of light defines what you see. The rhythm of life changes according to the seasonal rhythm. The rhythm of moods changes with the rhythm of your environment. There is a rhythm in the nice and not-so-nice experiences of your life.

The Principle of Cause and Effect — Hermetic philosophy states that nothing happens by chance. Every event is a result of cause and effect. Every cause has an effect, and every effect has a cause. There are many planes of causation. This law governs everything and everyone, and nothing can escape it.

The cosmos does not work on chance. Chances are only mental labels given to events or experiences whose cause cannot be deciphered or recognized. In the absence of chance, you have a different perspective on life. You look at events in your life and your experiences differently. Why did I fall sick? Why did I do this and not that? Why was I hurt by someone's remark? As you delve deep into your mind for answers to these questions, you get to understand your life better.

The Principle of Gender — Feminine and masculine aspects are in everything, and gender manifests on all planes of existence. At the physical level, the most obvious manifestation of gender is sex. According to Hermeticism, the negative pole (in the Principle of Polarity) is female, and the positive pole is male. It is important to know that negative and positive poles have nothing to do with negativity and positivity. It only means that the principle of gender is also apparent within the principle of polarity.

The female principle is associated with creativity, passivity, receiving, and imagination. The male principle is about willpower and material possession. The male and female principles have to work together for the cosmos to function. The two cannot work independently of each other.

These seven principles form the substance and framework of Hermeticism. When you see the world around you through these principles, your level of understanding of the world and yourself improves significantly. It helps you look at your experiences in more meaningful ways than before, and you find yourself living an increasingly fulfilling life.

Chapter 3: Principle #1: All is Mind

From this chapter onward, each of the seven principles of Hermeticism will be discussed in detail.

The Kybalion says, "*The one who understands the truth of the mental nature of the cosmos is far ahead on his or her path of mastery.*"

The first principle is the "Principle of Mentality" or "All is Mind." Hermeticism's key philosophical element reveals the true nature of matter, energy, and power. Using this Hermetic principle, it is possible to gain knowledge-driven power at the mental and psychic planes and use these lessons intelligently and wisely in your life.

Just as the "All Mind" creates its multiple universes, you create your universe using your creative mind, which is an extension of the one Creator or Life Force. Since you are a part of the Creator force with a powerful mind, you also have the innate mental and divine capabilities to bring about changes in your life as you wish.

This is why you must study the sacred universal laws to empower yourself and wake up your divine potential. Knowing the power of the All Mind of which your mind is a part will help you harness your full capabilities and create the life of your choice and desire. Hermeticism's ancient principles are the steppingstones to manifesting your life the way you want it to be.

According to the Principle of Mentality, the reality you experience, see, and sense are all based on mental ideas and concepts. Quantum physics defines mentalism as a concept through which the physical world is and can be changed/altered and drawn into potential connections and patterns through the application of consciousness. This idea is the same as the first Hermetic principle, which places consciousness above energy and matter. This rule applies to all three planes because everything is in the mind of the ALL.

Mental Alchemy also uses this theory and talks about transforming mental states and others through the power of the mind by changing beliefs and thoughts and expanding the mind. Making mental states changes can result in multiple benefits and help you navigate difficult patches easily and effectively.

Changing your thoughts and beliefs is not easy because any change is challenging and identifying your current state of mind and thought processes are difficult to achieve. Why is it difficult to understand your present state of mind? Here are a couple of easily relatable reasons:

Most people make the mistake of accepting their beliefs as the actual truth. Beliefs are embedded in your subconscious mind, which is frequently in conflict with your thoughts, which are in your conscious mind. You see what you believe.

Even modern neurological science gives proof of this. The human brain cannot differentiate between what it experiences and what it imagines experiencing. Both actual and imagined experiences trigger the same electrical patterns in the brain. The electrical connections and patterns reflect the way brains store and process data, including beliefs. You can change your beliefs by simply using your imagination.

Other tenets in Hermeticism that reflect the Principle of Mentality include:

The Law of One — Everyone is part of God, a single source of universal energy, and because of this, everyone is God too. With this power, people can manifest the love of God to one and all. This is the Law of One. It means that people are ALL one, and what they think, say, and do impacts every other soul.

Every soul is connected with the collective cosmic consciousness. The primary aim of life is to move toward and merge with this universal consciousness. When you live harmoniously with nature, you enhance your vibrational frequency, which drives you closer to God, and when in conflict with nature, your vibrational frequency decreases.

When you live according to the Law of One, you gain the fruits of the spirit and wisdom and knowledge by continuously applying the universal laws and Hermetic principles in your daily life. Living in this way helps you accept yourself and everyone and everything in this cosmos without judgment.

The Law of Self — This law states that finding yourself is the most important goal of your life. It shows that you come first in your world, and you should treat yourself this way. The Law of Self teaches you to accept that you are neither superior nor inferior but equal to everyone else. The degree to which you know and love yourself is the degree to which you know and love others. Here are important tenets in the Law of Self:

   • You are as much a part of the ALL and as divine as anyone else.

   • Your needs and wants are as vital as those of anyone else.

   • Taking care of yourself takes priority over taking care of anything or anyone else.

The Law of Self teaches you to give yourself to any activity or belief only up to the point when your spiritual, emotional, and physical energy begins to deplete. When anything you do depletes energy at these three levels, it means you are moving in a direction opposite to what you believe is right or doing something in conflict with another aspect of your life.

Regardless of why your energy is depleting, it translates to dishonoring the divinity within. It means you have replaced divinity with something or someone else, which is against the Law of Self. Honoring yourself is not being selfish. Now, you will look at the two parts of the Principle of Mentality or Mentalism, namely the psychology and the science aspects.

The Psychology of Mentalism

The psychology of mentalism deals with the idea that everything that is happening is in the mind. Everything that happens is a result of your mental state and how your mind perceives it. Here is a very fundamental example. When you see a table, what do you see? Just a table, right? How does your mind interpret the table?

The mind of the viewer comes into play. For instance, depending on the person viewing the table, what they see can differ from how someone else views it. One person might see the color of the table. Another might think it is a large, chunky one. A third person might look at the shape of it and choose to like it or dislike it. A fourth person could see it as something they always wanted in their dining room.

You can see that various layers of thoughts and ideas come up in the viewer's mind, depending on their mental state. You can see that once the object passes through the human brain, the table becomes much more than a simple table. It becomes what the viewer wants to see it as.

Mentalism's psychology can be understood further by the idea that whatever you see is colored by your perceptions, beliefs, thoughts, etc. It is as if you are viewing the world through a pair of colored spectacles, which makes you perceive things the way you choose to see them. The feelings you get from these perceptions form the basis of each of your realities.

An essential part of being a human being is trying to get back to the ultimate truth of the matter, which is achievable by emptying your mind. Meditation is a classic way to get back to the truth of the matter because it helps you perceive things without judgment and any rose-colored glasses.

When you see the ultimate truth, you find it easy to be balanced, grounded, and less impacted by your experiences and the things happening in your world. Meditation helps you reset your mind to the point of nothingness or emptiness, after which you can take a fresh perspective of everything around you.

Your biological eyes view things and send perceptions to your brain, which interprets your perceptions using stored data and thoughts. If the interpretation did not exist, there would be nothingness. Thoughts result in interpretation, and without these thoughts, there will not be any interpretation.

A great analogy of such a concept is dreaming. When you dream, you see yourself doing things, walking around, using your hands to do tasks, etc., when you know that you are not really doing anything because you are in bed lying down and your arms are resting next to your body.

A similar thing is believed in Hermeticism. That you are living in a dream, in an illusion, this is conflicting, right? A dream is a dream, whereas reality is not. Well, you know a dream is a dream only when you wake up, correct? In the same way, you need to "wake up" by empowering your mind to the ultimate truth: to see that you are in a "dream," and everything is in your mind.

According to quantum physics, everything in the cosmos comprises particles of energy, including your body, a chair, a table, and everything else around you. Imagine you are a character in a video game. What do you see? Pixelated images of yourself, right? When science advances so much that a scientist can get into your particles of energy, they will, perhaps, see reality as pixilated images too.

Mental means everything perceived is the mind. It is important not to worry when you hear such a description of your life—that everything is in your mind and imagination and you are alone. That is not the way to see the Principle of Mentality. Your life and your life experiences are not to be negated. They exist, and they empower your individuality.

The first Hermetic principle is based on the concept that everyone experiences things differently based on their minds and perceptions. Even if two people see the same thing, the experiences and perceptions are different and unique. Everyone is part of the "All Mind."

All that you see around you, including human beings, animals, plants, and everything, are merely concentrated energy points, all emanating from this "All Mind" or the Infinite Living Mind. This idea is quite deep and might take a bit of time to understand and grasp the crux of the matter. This ancient thought has been in existence for centuries now, and even modern science, especially in the area of quantum physics, appears to have found proof that the cosmos might be working in our minds.

The Science of Mentalism

The double-slit experiment is one of the most enlightening experiments of modern science, and the observations made appear to be aligned with the Principle of Mentality. What was seen in the double-slit experiment? Photons were passed through a two-slit screen. If the slits were observed, it looked like the photons passed through them like particles, one after the other. However, if the slits were not observed, it looked like the photons behaved like waves and simultaneously passed through both slits.

In 1978, John Wheeler, the famous theoretical physicist, proposed certain thought experiments using the double-slit setup. He proposed that observing the photons should only take place after they were emitted from their source. These thought experiments would take into account the effects of the observer on the outcome.

Take an example of what John Wheeler proposed to enhance the understanding of this concept. Suppose it was possible to close or open one of the slits after the photons were emitted from the source. If the interference pattern is still observed when the second slit is opened, you can conclude that the observer's decisions affect the photons' behavior.

In 2007, Alain Aspect and his teammates at French institutes, including the National Centre for Scientific Research, the Institut d'Optique, and Ecole Normale Supérieure de Cachan, performed the theoretical experiment that John Wheeler had thought of in 1978. In this experiment, the wave-particle duality was clearly seen.

Quantum mechanics states that all quantum objects could behave either as particles or waves, depending on the observer's perception. These observations demonstrated that the atoms seemed to know what the observer wanted to see and behaved accordingly.

Hermeticism also states the same thing through the Principle of Mentalism. The Unified Field or the "All Mind" everyone functions in is a collection of infinite probabilities. Moreover, what you perceive is one of these infinite probabilities that is picked out from your mental state and the manner of your perception.

Realities do not happen. They wait for your consciousness to interact. Depending on your experiences, decisions, and realities, they will then take place in our lives. The Unified Field is made of waves of probable outcomes waiting to happen, and the one you choose happens. Your mental interactions cause the outcomes you want.

The Law of Attraction and the Principle of Mentality or Mentalism

The Principle of Mentality states that you can manifest your reality for yourself. The thoughts and feelings you hold in your mind dictate what happens to you. This concept is in deep unity with the Law of Attraction. If you have an underlying vibration connected to a deep desire, this thought will manifest itself in your reality. It is as if the universe is working to help you achieve what you want, which is what the law of attraction is all about.

For example, suppose you feel anxious about tripping on the road on the way to work or something banging into you while you walk on the pavement. These experiences likely manifest in your reality. You can look back at your life and these seemingly weird experiences where you thought of something, and that thing happened. All these are classic, real-life examples of the first Hermetic principle.

When you realize that the cosmos is mental and everything happening around you is in your mind, you are essentially unlocking limitless potential abilities in your life. The realization takes time to sink into your subconscious mind because it is a very deep concept. But once this empowering belief sinks in, you can access many benefits, including:

• Becoming a psychic because you know consciously and intrinsically that everyone is from the same infinite energy source.

• Become a healer because of your increased ability to empathize with the sick person.

• Become a great influencer because of your capability to pass on and connect your thoughts with those of others.

Knowing and embracing the first Hermetic principle's power and knowledge will empower you to know that every other person is YOU because everyone comes from the same source. There is no separateness, just one being. You will have few premonitions, especially of those who are close to you. You can see the future as you see the past through your memories.

Lastly, the most important lesson in Hermeticism is that nothing can be learned instantly. It takes a lot of time to read, understand, and acknowledge the truth of Hermetic principles. You have started with the first one in the hope that it kindles your interest, so you continuously contemplate and meditate on the idea.

Moreover, the "All Mind" is limitless and unknowable. How much more difficult will it be to understand and know this all-encompassing power that cannot really be described using your limited vocabulary? Well, take lessons slowly and steadily, and persist in the learning. You will hit the jackpot when you are ready.

Also, try to implement this principle and its outcome in your daily life. Look at everything around you with new eyes. What do you see? Why do you see what you do? What are your feelings when you see it? Does the object look different when you have shifted your perspective?

Talk to yourself as much as you can, delve deep into your mind to find answers that already exist there because, after all, you are part of the Infinite Mind.

Chapter 4: Principle #2: As Above, So Below

The second Hermetic principle is the "Principle of Correspondence," which is considered the most popular. Although the tenets and thoughts found in the seven chapters of the Kybalion are believed to be thousands of years old, they can be applied to explain modern scenarios. The trick is to keep an open mind while trying to understand them.

The principle of correspondence states that there is always a correspondence between the laws and events taking place in the three planes of existence, namely the physical, mental, and spiritual. The Kybalion quote that expresses this principle the best is, *"As above, so below; as below, as above."*

This principle is also similar to the Arcane axiom, *"From one know all."* This means that all planes of existence function within the same framework of rules and patterns. It is possible to know the unknown by focusing on the known.

The principle of correspondence states that the physical, mental, and spiritual planes work harmoniously with each other. Everything in this cosmos is connected and in correspondence with everything else. What is within you is outside of you, which means the macrocosm (the larger world) is in the microcosm (the smaller world), and vice versa.

Actual or Literal Reality

The solar systems, life on earth, societies, the human body, plants, animals, and everything else are harmoniously connected with and influence each other. For example, there are patterns in nature similar to each other despite being separated by incredibly large distances. Here are several excellent examples, as seen and photographed using advanced scientific equipment:

The birth of a cell looks similar to the death of a star.

The helix of a nebula looks a lot like the human eye.

The universe looks similar to the nerve network in the human brain.

With the planets revolving around the sun, the solar system looks like an atom with electrons revolving around protons.

The formation of the universe looks similar to neurons under the microscope.

The Milky Way galaxy and the picture of a hurricane taken from space have startling resemblances.

The Fibonacci sequence can also be seen in multiple natural creations, including flowers, plants, arrangements of stars in the sky, and many other elements in the micro and macro world. These examples are excellent proof that laws remain the same regardless of the scale and plane of existence. According to Hermeticism, these startling similarities prove that everything was created from the same source and using the same framework of laws.

Personal or Individual Reality

Your beliefs, feelings, and thoughts manifest your reality. So, the reality you experience right now is exactly the way you have chosen to manifest it. Here, too, the law of attraction comes into play.

For example, if, for any reason, you look at the outside world as unkind and cruel, it is a reflection of your inner feelings and thoughts. This "unkind, cruel" reality you experience is caused by how you see things through a rose-colored lens via your feelings and thoughts. You attract the same vibration that you hold within you. What is within corresponds to what is outside.

So, as mentioned earlier, to change the outer world, you need to heal and work on your inner world. That is why people take the path of spirituality and heal their inner selves so that the outer world corresponds to the changed perception. When you heal yourself of past pains, hurts, victimizations, and other negative emotions, you change your perception of the outer world. Your reality undergoes positive changes as well.

It is important to question the beliefs and ideas that have been given to you and make appropriate changes within yourself. In the same way, look at your thoughts. Ask yourself why you think of and perceive certain things in a certain way. Can you change the way you look at it? And when you change that, the observed thing takes on a new look in your experience.

Another inner world aspect that can change your outer world is your core belief that you have been indoctrinated with by your culture. For example, do you believe that boys should be like this and girls should be like that? Or do you feel that you cannot achieve certain goals because of your gender, race, or any other limiting factor? If yes, then you need to question it and ask yourself if this is correct or not.

The thing to remember is that the core beliefs of your inner self impact your outer world experiences. If and when you shift your inner world beliefs, your outer world changes correspondingly, which is what the principle of correspondence is all about.

What you do at each individual level will find its impact at the macro level too. Even the smallest behaviors and acts impact the grand scheme of things in the entire cosmos. It works like the butterfly effect, where doing any little thing can greatly impact your life and the world around you.

This second Hermetic principle means that your outer world is a reflection of your inner world. The images and thoughts in your conscious and subconscious minds find a way to appear in the external world. This situation can lead to confusion because it becomes difficult to distinguish between reality, faith, and illusion. It confuses facts with our opinions. Also, the world around you is made exactly the way you want it.

The outer world is a reflection of your inner world. So, look at the surrounding beauty, including the light, love, joy, and wonder around you, and this becomes your inner reflection. This holds good for the not-so-good aspects of life too. Whatever you consider bad in you will be seen as bad in others too. If you do not find the courage to face your demons and fears, these shadows will appear in the people around you because the outer world reflects what is within you.

Hermeticism says that the inner world is the cause and what you see and experience in the outer world are the effects. So, if the effects have to be changed, the causes have to be changed. If you perceive chaos and lack of love in the outer world, it means your inner world is also chaotic, and there is no love.

The way to control the outer world is to control your inner world. Look within you, solve your internal problems, and the external world's problems will take care of themselves. The second Hermetic principle empowers you to stop looking for excuses for your problems. Instead, it helps you realize that real answers are available by looking within.

Modern Perspective of the Principle of Correspondence

You already know the Hermetic axiom, *"As above, so below; as below, so above,"* means what is within is without and vice versa. In this scenario, the "above" refers to the macrocosm or the "All Mind," the World Soul or the spiritual plane. The "without" refers to the "reality" you experience in this world where you live, eat, sleep, pay bills, meet deadlines, and interact with other people.

Also, the "without" can be thought of as your "landscape," and the "within" as your "dreamscape" or inner world, the place you are when you dream or meet your inner self, ego, or other "inner characters." This concept can be quite baffling for most people in the modern world, considering they are so deeply immersed in a rationalist, materialist perspective of the world. The second Hermetic principle has two important points that differ from the modern worldview.

The first point is that this law recognizes the three planes of existence: the spiritual, mental, and physical, and each vibrate at a different frequency. The densest, slowest, and the coarsest plane is the physical one, which is made up of matter. The fastest plane and the one with the finest vibration is the spiritual world. These three planes are interconnected, and a situation in one impacts events and experiences in the other two.

For example, if you want to get insights into your spiritual reality, you can examine your physical and mental world elements, such as your health, wealth, and feelings. On the contrary, if you need to understand the cause of your health issues, you can examine your spiritual reality for insights into your physical problems.

The second point to understanding the second Hermetic principle better is based on the concept of "unus mundus" or "all is one" or the "unity of all things." Therefore, something apparently unrelated to another could influence it in seemingly unimaginable ways. If you look at it like this, the human body is the microcosm of the world, which is the macrocosm. Each individual's soul is connected to the world soul (or the "All Mind").

Alchemists use seven metals in their laboratory: lead, tin, iron, gold, mercury, copper, and silver—in that order. This order is connected to the Ptolemaic system of seven planets in the following way:

Lead — Lead is governed by Saturn and is believed to be related to transformation and death. Burning lead removes its impurities and is metaphorical to cleansing and removing the imperfections of human beings. Lead, one of the earliest known metals, was also associated with divination spells.

Tin — Tin is governed by Jupiter and embodies logic, wisdom, maturity, education, and knowledge. Tin is believed to be the metal of scholars and sages and is associated with philosophy, mediation, and balance. It is also related to prosperity and wealth.

Iron — Iron is one of the most abundant elements found in the universe and is governed by Mars. It is connected to aggression, physical power, growth, protection, and symbolizes masculine energy. It promotes emotions like confidence, lust, courage, stamina, strength, and resilience. Interestingly, iron is believed to be the most "human" metal and is not trusted by spirits and other ethereal entities.

Gold — Gold is governed by the Sun and symbolizes purity and perfection. This is why it was offered to the gods and used for ceremonial purposes, jewelry, and other embellishments. Gold is seen as a symbol of authority, prosperity, and charisma.

Mercury — The metal mercury is associated with the planet Mercury. It is an unusual metal because it exists in liquid form at room temperature. It's a toxic metal connected to mystery, death, and transformation. It's also connected to divination and used in spells related to movement and travel, both physical and spiritual. Alchemists considered mercury to be one of the three principal elements on earth—the other two being sulfur and salt.

Copper — Copper is ruled by Venus and embodies the nurturing and nourishing aspect of women. It is associated with love, lust and stands for feminine beauty, charism, artistic creativity, caring, affection, and balance. It is also believed to have healing properties.

Silver — Silver is governed by the moon and one of the three base metals in alchemy, thanks to its versatility. It is related to intuition, inner wisdom, and self-reflection. A feminine metal, silver is connected to spirits and goddesses and is a symbol of purity. This metal's energies are highly effective in healing, divination, emotion, protection, wisdom, dreams, and luck.

These seven metals were also related to the ages of humans, zodiac signs, and more. The planets were also used in astrology as their position at the time of a person's birth gave insights into the individual's life, challenges, talents, and destiny. The ancients recognized the various planes of existence in this way.

Interestingly, Carl Jung, the famous psychoanalyst and psychiatrist, appreciated and drew upon these interconnections among the planes and used them to formulate his ideas. He studied the *Corpus Hermeticum* to derive information and inspiration for insights into the modern world of psychoanalysis and psychiatry.

Jung openly admitted his respect for Hermetic wisdom and recognized the healing powers of the ancient Hermetic's holistic approach to cure sickness by curing the affected individual's soul. He argued against the suppression of psychic premises held in Hermetic philosophy simply for the sake of "scientific objectivity."

The Law of Correspondence can also be interpreted like this. Every cell within your body contains your entire being, and your entire being contains the entire cosmos. Everything around you and in this universe is a reflection of you. The second Hermetic principle is believed to hold the deepest truth in the universe. To reiterate, "*As below, so below; as below, so above. As within, so without; as without, so within.*" Everything is in correspondence with everything else in this vast cosmos because everyone is from the same source and shares the same patterns.

Chapter 5: Principle #3: The Principle of Vibration

The third Hermetic principle, referred to as the Principle of Vibration, states that everything in the universe continuously vibrates and moves. Nothing rests. This is true for the tiniest molecule known to human beings to the largest rock in all the three planes of existence.

There is vibration in sound, light, matter, and energy. Physics explains two kinds of vibration (often called oscillation by physicists). One type is the pendulum-like forward-backward movement, and the second type is random vibrations. Any vibration can be described using three factors:

- The amplitude or size of vibration.
- The frequency or rate of vibration.
- The phase or timing of vibration.

Hermetics and other occultists believe that the differences in these three factors determine the different planes of existence, with the spiritual plane vibration at the highest rate. Also, every emotional and/or mental state can be defined by its vibration rate, and the individual skilled enough to know can control and influence others at their will.

Interestingly, modern scientific studies confirm this constant state of motion of all things in the universe, something that the ancient wise Hermetic sages enunciated thousands of years ago. The ancient Hermetics stated that the differences in various elemental manifestations are dependent on the differing vibration rates.

Everything is in vibration from the "All Mind" or the Pure Spirit up to the grossest matter. The higher the vibration of an element, the higher its position in the scale of existence. The spirit element's vibration is at such an infinite speed and intensity that it appears to rest. This is similar to a rapidly moving wheel that looks stationary.

At the other end of the spectrum are the gross forms of matter whose vibrations are so slow that they also appear to be at rest. Between these two extreme ends, there exists an infinite number of different degrees of vibration. Using this principle, Hermetics believes it is possible to change your mental state by changing your thoughts' vibration. Another interesting point to note in Hermetic philosophy is that the principle of vibration is deeply connected to the principles of polarity and rhythm.

Empaths are naturally inclined to read and connect with the vibrations of their surroundings. Even those who do not believe they are empaths can learn to read and analyze the vibrations in an environment. This ability to read is primarily based on the Hermetic concept of the principle of vibration that everything in this cosmos is in a constant change of flux. Who can read the strength of vibrations is dependent on many other factors, including the individual's intuitive powers.

So, why does everything vibrate? According to Hermeticism, the reason why everything vibrates at its own frequency is that everything is energy. For example, if you see a pillow, you see just a physical entity. As you delve deep into the third principle of Hermetic philosophy, you will realize that the seemingly at-rest pillow is vibrating at its own frequency that it is so dense and gross that it appears to rest. The reason why everyone perceives differently is because they read the surrounding vibrations differently.

If you were to read religious books on your own without depending on the teachings of someone who (owing to being a different person from you will interpret the teachings differently), you will see that all religions of the world say the same thing. Everyone is from the same source; even the names of the divine sources change according to religion.

The lesson on vibration is important because once you realize that all things in the universe are moving at a particular frequency, this will help you achieve your desires by aligning the frequency of your goals to attract similar frequencies into your life.

You might have felt great, positive vibes with certain people, and with others, the vibes might not have been so great. These feelings are nothing but the connection of your vibration with that of the other person. If the frequencies are aligned, you feel a great vibe. If the frequencies are misaligned or on opposite sides, you feel a negative vibe. Many people can connect with the vibrations of neighboring people.

Similarly, if you put your mind to it, you can sense the vibrations and the frequencies of vibrations of everything and everyone in the world, which can enhance your life positively.

While it is true that all things in the cosmos vibrate at varying frequencies, it is important to note that the speed of vibration does not make it good or bad. The only thing to note is that the lower the vibration's frequency, the denser the thing is. Physical planes and the elements in them vibrate at low speeds.

Even within the physical plane, each element vibrates at a unique frequency. For example, crystals, gemstones, etc., vibrate differently from a more common element like a pillow, wardrobe, etc. Within the human body, each organ, tissue, and cell vibrate at slightly different vibrations. When the frequencies of the two things are different from each other, the two never meet. When the frequencies of the two elements are close enough, it is possible to pick up each other's frequencies.

You can take the analogy of a radio station to understand this concept. If you are listening to a radio show at 99.1, you can pick up signals of 98.3 or something closer. You are unlikely to pick up a 93.3 or 104 frequency; the vibrational frequencies of everything in this universe work in the same way. Every different dimension vibrates at a different frequency, and every little presence in these dimensions also vibrates at different frequencies. Matching the vibrations of your desires with your actions is essential to living a meaningful and fulfilling life.

One of the best things about knowing and understanding the principle of vibration is that you can use it to make changes in your life by changing vibration frequency. It is possible to sit in one place and adjust your mental and emotional frequency to match higher plane frequencies and travel to these planes without moving your physical body.

So, how does one raise vibrations? While there are multiple ways you can do this, using emotions is one of the most powerful tools to raise your vibrations. In fact, emotions are the GPS that helps people understand their mental state. Here is a simple experiment you can try to raise your vibration.

Imagine the source of your divinity. Ask yourself who you truly are. Remind yourself that the human body holds a part of the "All Mind," a concept discussed in the Principle of Mentalism, a part referred to as the soul or spirit. Now, imagine your body is connected with your soul. Imagine an anchor dropped into the soul.

Keep this image in your mind, and as you go about living your daily, routine life encountering bad and good experiences, know that this connection or anchor, something that works like a bungee jumping roping, is pulling you toward your core spirit. Also, know that the further away you go from this seat of Oneness or the part of the

"All Mind," which is your own divinity, the more resistance you feel within yourself.

This resistance, which you will experience both emotionally and physically, causes negative emotions and conflicts in your mind. The further away you go from your divinity, the more the resistance and negativity is in your life. The opposite is also true. The closer you get to your divinity or spiritual center, the less resistance you feel within yourself, and you experience much positivity.

As you get closer to your spiritual center, you feel a sense of calmness pervading within you, a sense of relief that you are where you should be. As the distance from your divinity decreases, you feel a sense of hope, and you move from feeling pessimistic to optimistic about everything in your life.

Even emotions vibrate at different frequencies, and it is possible to move from one emotion to another by raising your frequency of thought. It's vital to note that moving from negative to positive emotions takes time and persistent practice. Even a small movement toward improved emotion management is good, and as you persist, you get closer to your goals.

Now use the radio station frequency again to understand this. Suppose 99.1 represents frustration. With a little effort, you can move to 98.3, which would perhaps represent apathy or indifference. This movement from frustration to apathy is good progress, and from 98.3, you can slowly pick-up different frequencies that are closer to positivity.

It is important to note that moving from one end of the emotional spectrum to the other is achievable. If you manage to do it, the transformation will not be sustained because when you move swiftly from one emotion to another, you are likely to miss out on the various perceptions at each transformation, leaving your lessons half-learned and inadequate. You must take one small step at a time and move toward positivity by changing your thoughts and ideas.

Every day make a conscious effort to focus on your thoughts. What are you thinking? What are you feeling? These thoughts and feelings, which are quite interrelated, determine your vibrational frequency. Conversely, if you consciously notice the manifestations in your life, and see negative things happening in it, now you should know that these experiences are a result of your inner vibrations. The reason for the manifestations is that you have been vibrating in that frequency for a long time. This happens regardless of whether the manifestation is good or bad.

Since everything is energy coming from the same source (All Mind), there is really no difference between your thoughts and the external world. The only difference is in the degree of vibration. So, if you take two human beings living together, both are elements of the same god-energy vibrating at different frequencies—that is all. The relationship between the two is the result of the combination of individual frequencies.

This world is focused or concentrated on energy or thought. Suppose you vibrate at a particular frequency because of one thought that is going through your mind. If you can keep this thought, you continue to vibrate at that same frequency. Additionally, you attract other elements that vibrate at the same frequency. The focus of this thought gets so strong that it manifests itself physically in some form.

So, you can use this concept to your advantage. If you have a deep desire (which is also a form of energy vibrating at a particular frequency), sit with that desire and allow your body and mind to imbibe it so that there is increased focus on that energy. If you are unsure of your desires, simply start with one good thought. Keep that thought in your mind for seventeen seconds because it is believed that it takes about seventeen seconds for a thought to begin vibrating at a faster level, which, in turn, will attract other thoughts whose vibrations are aligned with this good thought.

Once you get this exercise started, you practice persistently and keep thinking good thoughts. Your life is bound to see significant improvements because of the ever-increasing inflow of frequencies similar to good thoughts and their subsequent manifestations.

When spells are used in magical rituals, this is exactly what is being done. The energy that is in sync with the vibration of the seeker's desire is brought to the present moment by the witch or any other practitioner to be manifested right away. Any magician's, witch's, or alternative practitioner's primary goal is to master the art of matching vibrational frequencies. This is achieved by conquering and controlling their own minds and emotions.

Interestingly, as you practice Hermeticism and its various principles, and particularly the third one, you will realize that emotions can be used as tools to manage your life and life experiences effectively. Emotion is more than something that merely needs to be controlled, manipulated, or kept in check. Instead, you will learn through experience that emotions help you decipher your present state of mind and the cause of that state. Emotions are efficient measuring tools.

For example, if you feel guilty, it reflects a thought or action you have taken. So, immediately, you can stop for a while, look at the underlying thought, and see why and how that emotion came into play. You can then do things that change this thought or vibration, and consequently, change the way you feel.

On the other hand, if you feel happy or pleasant, you can examine the underlying thought and work at keeping that thought going to sustain the good feelings in your system.

How to Raise Your Vibrations

So, now that you know your vibrations determine the manifestations in your life, it makes sense to find out how you can raise them to improve your overall wellbeing.

Be Conscious of Your Thoughts — Every thought, word, and feeling becomes your reality, provided they are focused enough to manifest themselves. For years, many people live with limiting beliefs like they must do this or that because they have been "coached" or "trained" by the society, culture, family, etc., they live in.

Suppose you are a woman and want to follow your desire for something that has been historically associated with men. In that case, you could choose not to follow that desire because you have been told that it is not for you, and the thought *I cannot do this because I am a woman* is deeply embedded in your psyche.

Alternatively, if you are a man and want to do something historically seen as being feminine, you could choose not to follow that path because of that limiting thought. Now, recognize and be conscious of such limiting thoughts and acknowledge their impact on the manifestations. The first step is to acknowledge your thoughts and then move on to finding ways to change them.

Appreciate the beauty around you—many people unwittingly forget to see the immense beauty of life and the cosmos that is all around them. People are so caught up in their lives and problems that they end up living with blinders on. Find a little time every day to pause as you rush from one task to another to look at and appreciate the abundant beauty.

Simply stand in the sun and bask in its warmth. Look at a flower closely and wonder at the beauty of creation. A positive action, even for a brief time, can raise your vibrations as you connect with the vibrations of the beautiful things in your life.

Drink Plenty of Water — Sufficient quantities of good, clean, fresh water are vital for removing toxins from your body. If these toxins accumulate in your body, they tend to lower your vibrations.

Be Conscious of What You Consume — Foods also have a vibration. Organically grown fresh fruit and vegetables vibrate at a higher frequency than processed foods. Foods that are grown using chemicals and pesticides or wrapped in plastic vibrate at a lower frequency, which is not good for you. Natural foods imbibe the high frequencies that nature bestows on them, and it would be good for you to eat these foods.

Live in Gratitude — Shifting your focus from your troubles to an attitude of gratitude helps you to appreciate what you have instead of worrying about what you do not. Not only that, being grateful enhances your vibrations and attracts high-frequency, positive elements into your life. You end up having more things to show gratitude for.

Meditate Every Day — A simple meditation technique works like this:

Sit comfortably in a quiet, undisturbed spot.

Close your eyes.

Breathe in and breathe out.

As you do so, focus on your nostrils and feel the breath as it enters and leaves your body.

Every time you notice your thoughts going somewhere else instead of your breath, gently bring the focus back to your nostrils and continue breathing. Start with just five minutes of this exercise. When you feel comfortable, increase the duration of meditation by another five minutes each week or as often as you like. Meditating calms your spirit and helps keep the negative impact of anxiety at bay, ensuring your vibrations are at a higher level.

Practice Kindness — Doing charity helps you realize that you are not the only person in the world suffering. Every human being is fighting their own battle. This knowledge makes you feel less lonely, and you feel empowered to live more positively than before, thereby raising your vibrations.

To summarize, the Hermetic principle of vibration is a powerful tool in your hands to take control of your life and make conscious efforts to alter the way you live so that you can attract all the good things in life and follow your dreams and desires uninhibitedly. To think that modern science is slowly proving the validity of ancient wisdom tells much about human ancestors who seemed to know far more about how to be happy with little. It is time to harness the power of ancient wisdom and live the life you deserve by raising your vibrations.

Chapter 6: Principle #4: There Are Two Sides to Everything

According to the Kybalion, everything has polarity and is dual. The fourth Hermetic principle states that everything has its pair of opposites. Opposites are identical in nature, only different in degrees and extremes. All truths are only half-truths, all paradoxes can be reconciled, and there are two sides to all things.

An easy analogy to understand this is your thermometer. Heat terminates where cold begins. There is nothing called "absolute cold" or "absolute heat." Heat and cold are both the same thing, only varying in degrees of vibration, so heat and cold are the two poles of what is commonly referred to as heat, and this manifestation is a classic example of the principle of polarity.

Similarly, light and darkness are two poles of the same thing, varying in degrees only. Darkness leaves where light begins. Large and small, soft and hard, black and white, dull and sharp, high and low, etc., are all poles that only vary in degree, not in nature. The principle of polarity works the same in the mental plane as well.

Take another example of the opposite in personality. Suppose there is an intuitive or emotional person, and another is mathematical or logical. Although there are no hard and fast rules to define personality perfectly, these two kinds of people are usually on the opposite sides of a personality spectrum.

Similarly, people are holistic or analytical. The former set of people look at things holistically while the latter look at each individual element of a situation and analyze it in detail. Again, these two kinds of people are at opposite poles. Although there are opposites, according to the fourth principle of Hermeticism, there are all the same things. Analytical and intuitive people are different degrees of personality, which is the same thing.

So it goes for optimistic and pessimistic people. They are of the same nature (it describes a way of thinking), and the two only differ in degrees. A pessimist responds or ignores certain elements, while optimists respond or ignore certain other elements because their perspectives change. Linear and circular might look different, but they are the same thing, which is how the line is drawn or described. Poles are merely illusions, and everything you think about is the same thing.

Now, look at one of the most common opposite pairs in emotion: love and hate. Most people know and believe that love and hate are two mental states that are seemingly completely different. Degrees of love and hate melt into each other so gradually that people sometimes cannot discern the difference.

For example, like and dislike are two degrees of love and hate that are so close to each other that often people find it difficult to decide whether they like or dislike something or someone or neither of the two. This is because both are degrees of the same thing and only differ in slight vibrational frequencies—and the extremes combine to form one idea or concept.

Another key factor to keep in mind is that there is a blurriness between the opposites. You could ask, "Where do the poles meet?" For example, at what point in this polarity scale does loud end and quietly begin or sharp end and blunt begin, and vice versa? The answer to this question is subjective as there is no clear defining point.

To take an example of blunt and sharp, if you looked at a knife and wanted to know if it was blunt or sharp, the observer's subjectivity comes into play. The knife could be sharp for a child, whereas the same knife could be blunt for a chef who uses it to cut vegetables or meat. Labeling and describing things is highly individualistic and depends on the person perceiving the object.

You can see that the fourth Hermetic principle implies that there are no absolutes in the world. Everything is relative to the observer. This is the basis of why it is vital not to be judgmental. Judging people, circumstances, or anything else is pointless because it is like clutching at straws. Considering the duality of everything and the blurriness between the poles, judging things or people is quite futile, and knowing and accepting this idea can make a big difference in the way you see yourself and the world around you.

One of the most important outcomes driven by the fourth Hermetic principle is that Hermeticism followers believe and accept that it is possible to change the vibrations of polarity both in their minds and in others' minds.

If you look back at your life, you can recall many instances where love rapidly transformed into hate, and many times, hate transformed into love. These common occurrences in most people's lives also prove the point of the Hermetic principle of polarity. If love and hate can be interchanged involuntarily, this change can be accomplished better when used willfully.

The principle of polarity also demonstrates that good and evil are also extreme poles of the same thing, and it is possible to transmit evil into good by applying this principle in life. The Kybalion says that you can use your willpower to destroy an undesirable rate of mental vibration by changing its polarity.

Modern psychologists use the principle of polarity to help their students and clients break undesirable habits by asking them to focus on the opposite quality. For example, if you are overcome by fear, instead of wasting time and energy to kill the fear, simply focus on its opposite pair, namely courage. Since the two are of the same thing, fear will be replaced by courage.

When you are in a dark room, it would be needless to try to shovel out the darkness. Instead, you simply allow light to enter, and the darkness automatically disappears. In the same way, let courage in to make fear disappear. In short, focus on the positive pole of a negative quality or habit to kill it out until you become polarized on the positive instead of the negative of the same thing.

It is important to know that the reverse is also true, especially if you allow yourself to vibrate at an element's negative pole, so you can master your moods and transform your mental states, and reconstitute your disposition, all of which will enhance your personality and character by changing your polarity. Teachings that reflect the Hermetic principle of polarity include:

- Every coin has two sides.

- There are no problems in this world, only solutions.

- The Law of Evolution.

The Law of Evolution

The first two axioms are easy to understand. Now, look at the law of evolution in more detail.

Transformation is the fundamental premise for evolution. Change is the core principle of evolution. If everything remains static, there would be no evolution. Also, the truth can be comprehended only through experience. According to the Hermetic laws, learning can never be denied or suppressed permanently. At some point in time, everything in this cosmos will be learned.

The Law of Evolution covers every single element and life in this cosmos. No one can escape it. Interestingly, this law is one of the most progressive ones globally, considering that it allows chaos to exist and promotes it. Changes and transformations bring about chaos, at the end of which lies an element that is more evolved than before the transformation. And this goes on endlessly.

It is best to accept and consciously make changes when transformation happens for an increased effect on your life. For example, if you are unhappy about anything in your life, you can determinedly alter your thoughts, beliefs, and actions to bring transformations you desire.

While deciding to change, you should consciously choose which of your misaligned beliefs you want to work with and transform. The interesting thing about changing your attitude toward something is that you do not need to change your feelings toward it. If you dislike something, you don't need to compel yourself to like it. However, you must be ready to shift your thoughts and perspectives about the thing so that evolution happens, and you find yourself in a better place regarding that disharmonious circumstance or person in your life.

Understanding Paradoxes and Transcending the Poles

A vital aspect of the principle of polarity is that all paradoxes can be reconciled. This is because of the Oneness regarding how everything comes from the same source of energy. The extreme poles combine to form one concept, and all concepts combine to form the All or the single Infinite Being that everything in this cosmos is a part of.

The ultimate purpose of everything is to rejoin with that Oneness from which everyone comes from. To do that, you must transcend the poles. It is important that you recognize and identify the spectrum of opposites and transcend them or see through them to discover the central All. When you transcend the opposites, you will realize the oneness of everyone and that people are different parts experiencing "differently" the same things.

So, how can you apply the principle of polarity in your daily life? The Law of One describes everyone being oriented to "service ourselves or others." Most often, people do things and live in ways that will be of service to themselves. Sometimes, they do things or take actions to be of service to those around them.

Suppose you direct your actions more toward the service of others. In that case, you tend to move toward Oneness because such acts drive you to behave as if you are an indivisible whole instead of being a separate individual. You see no boundaries between yourself and others. Yet, you must look after yourself, too, because if you are not at your full capacity, you will not be able to be of service to others. What is needed is to keep a good balance between looking after yourself and serving others.

Once you understand that it is possible to transcend the poles and see everything as part of the All, it is now time to try and avoid a polarized attitude, or at least how to work on not being overly attuned to the negative pole of all aspects in your life. The first step is in choosing a pole that lies more toward the positive end of the spectrum. For example, if you choose to be a nice person instead of a nasty one, your thoughts swing to the positive end automatically.

Knowing and acknowledging the principle of polarity allows you to become increasingly aware of your emotions and thoughts and choose to behave and embrace the polarity spectrum's positive side. There is increased self-awareness as you try to gauge and label your emotions. Are you at the positive or negative pole?

Through self-awareness, when you realize that you are at a pole you do not want to be in, you can change your vibrations and move away from it. With this increased self-awareness comes the urge to move and lean toward the positive pole, which, in turn, helps you connect with your inner divinity or the cosmic "All Mind."

The fourth Hermetic principle, which is the principle of polarity, teaches you to acknowledge and accept the duality of everything in this universe. It teaches that duality exists only in varying degrees and not in the nature of the thing. It also shows that you can choose your poles and improve your self-awareness. Moreover, Hermeticism's final aim is to regain your connection with the "All Mind," which is possible by transcending polarity.

Practical Applications of the Principle of Polarity

The practical application of the principle of polarity can be seen in a thought experiment of Erwin Schrodinger, a Nobel prize-winning quantum physicist whose name was cemented in the world of physics through this interesting theory he proposed.

So, what was the Schrodinger's Cat thought experiment all about? He proposed the following theoretical experiment in 1935. If a cat were placed in a closed box along with a Geiger counter, a vial of poison, a hammer, and a radioactive substance—all of which were connected to each other in a way that one reaction could trigger—a chain of events would follow:

When the Geiger counter detects the radioactive substance decaying, it will trigger the hammer to hit the vial, thereby releasing the poison. This poison would kill the cat. Now, the radioactive substance decaying is a random process. No one can predict the exact moment when it will happen.

According to physicists, atoms in a radioactive substance exist in a "superposition" state. A superposition state is defined as a state when both non-decayed and decayed atoms exist simultaneously.

With this condition, it is impossible to know if the cat is alive or dead until the box is opened and someone sees or observes it. Until then, the cat's life is connected to the radioactive substance and when it will decay to the extent that the Geiger counter can detect and trigger the hammer. Schrodinger proposed that, theoretically speaking, the cat is alive and dead in equal parts until the box is open.

Once the cat is observed, the "superposition" of the cat (being alive and dead in equal parts) would collapse, leaving behind one of either "the cat is dead" or "the cat is alive." This theoretical thought experiment was used to demonstrate that you cannot say anything is happening or not happening until you observe it. You can say it can be one of many things that could be happening, even if the probability is small. But you can never say that something has happened until after you observe it.

Hermeticism talks exactly of this perception of the observer. So, if you see a flower, another observer assumes you see the flower too. However, that observer does not know how this flower looks to you. Your consciousness is different from the second observer's consciousness, and the concept of perception between the two observers involves three worlds. Those are a "real world," which has the flower, your world, which has the flower as you perceive it, and the second observer's world with the flower as they perceive it.

The challenge here is that no one knows what the "real world" is. Therefore, the standard scientific definition of perception is limited to each individual's experience and nothing beyond that. Hermeticism believes that because of the individual's perceptions clouding your vision, you find it difficult to see that everyone is various aspects of the "All Mind." Schrodinger said the real essence of all phenomena in this cosmos is to track down the relations between your experience's various aspects. Through this, you achieve the Oneness from which everyone emerges.

The wise ancient Hermetics spoke of this Oneness thousands of years ago and said that everyone's manifestations are merely focused points of the All Mind. Understanding the polarities of all elements will help you bring together the extremes, which, when combined, become one again.

While it is impossible to control what is happening in the external world, it is possible to control and change the events when they come into your internal world's influence. Charles Swindoll, the famous evangelist, educator, and author, has an interesting quote to depict this concept, "Our life is 10% what happens to us, and 90% how we choose to react or respond to what happens to us."

Therefore, when you experience thoughts and emotions from either pole, you get the option to accept or reject each of those thoughts and emotions. Mental transmutation processes are heavily dependent on these options of whether you should accept or reject what is happening in your mind. Inner peace begins when you choose not to allow the external world's happenings to control your emotions and thoughts.

The choice to accept or reject what happens in your mind is entirely in your hands, and no one can really influence you to do their bidding unless you permit them to do so. When you are faced with choosing between the negative and the positive poles, your choice is the final choice. The knowledge of the principle of polarity empowers you to choose without depending on the external world.

Chapter 7: Principle #5: The Principle of Rhythm

According to the Kybalion, the fifth Hermetic principle goes as follows, *"Everything has its ups and downs. Everything flows in and out. The swing of the pendulum is manifested in all things in this cosmos. The swing to one side is equal to the swing to the other side. Rhythms compensate each other."* The last line of this opening paragraph is dealt with in the Law of Compensation later in this chapter.

The word "rhythm" is rooted in the Greek word "rhuthmos," which means symmetrical measured movement or flow. Rhythm is the variation of the accentuation and length of a series of events or vibrations. So, what does the fifth principle in Hermeticism really mean? It says some deep things about reality. It says that reality works on an algorithm, a predefined set of rules and processes to be followed in your life's calculations.

The rhythm tends to swing between the two poles as defined in the Principle of Polarity. So, it swings from happy to sad, from light to darkness, from right to left, from success to failure, etc. There is recurring change, activity, and motion in a rhythm. Universes are created through the Outpouring of the All Mind. These created universes reach the lowest point of their materiality and then begin their journey inward to be absorbed back into the All Mind through the Indrawing.

Similarly, stars and suns are powered into existence, and after reaching the peak of their powers, they begin the journey of regression and slowly and surely become dead matter until they are empowered with new energy where a new cycle begins. Rhythm perpetuates the concept of time, and history repeats itself. Everything goes and comes back in rhythm. Rhythm permits change and transitions. It shows the existence of two opposites.

The rhythm of sound is the most apparent in human life. Another classic example of a natural rhythm is the "Circadian rhythm," which is the daily cycle of all living beings' behavioral, biochemical, and physiological processes, including plants, animals, fungi, bacteria, and human beings. You can see rhythm in the following aspects of the cosmos:

- Within atoms, as they vibrate rhythmically.
- Within the movement of heavenly bodies, like planets and natural satellites.
- Within the moon's waxes and wanes.
- With the alternating seasons.
- Within philosophies and creeds.
- Within the cycle of night and day.
- Within the changing tides.
- Within breathing.

The above illustrations are not exhaustive in any way. Everything in existence is always in a dance. Everything in this world and the entire universe has rhythm, and this is the fifth Hermetic principle. This rhythm can be in any form, including but not limited to:

- An action and a reaction.
- An advance and a retreat.

- A rising and ebbing or sinking.

This law of rhythm is seen everywhere and in everything. It can be seen in the creation and destruction of the worlds, in life and death, in the rise and fall of civilizations and nations, and even in human beings' mental states. There is no concept of absolute rest or total cessation from movement. The fifth principle is universal and can be applied to any question or phenomenon in any plane of existence. The universal pendulum is in eternal motion, and the tides of life flow in and out. Rhythm is also seen in the mind, which is one of the most important practical applications of the fifth Hermetic principle in people's daily lives.

Learning and mastering the dynamics of rhythm can help ease some of its severe negative impacts. If you learn to stay in the flow of the rhythm, your life can be smooth. The Hermetics have acknowledged, learned, and mastered this principle and have also found ways and means to overcome the negative effects of this mental and emotional rhythm. Through the fifth principle's knowledge, Hermetics have learned to use it effectively in their lives instead of being used by it.

In the mental phenomena, the ancient Hermetics realized that there were two planes of consciousness: the Higher and the Lower. This understanding helped the wise Hermetics to rise to the higher consciousness, which, in turn, helped them escape the swing of the pendulum in its return trip in the lower plane. The Hermetics called this the Law of Neutralization.

They raised their ego above their mental activity's vibrations so that the negative swing was not manifested in their consciousness. This approach is analogous to rising above something so that it can pass beneath you without affecting you. Using the Mental Law of Neutralization, a master Hermetic, or an advanced student, would polarize themselves to the point on the polarity scale at which they want to rest. They neutralize the rhythmic effect by raising their vibrations to a higher plane when the pendulum swing takes the individual to the other pole in equal measure.

This process was similar to "deliberately" not participating in the negative swing of the pendulum. Nearly all individuals who have learned the art of self-mastery would achieve this by not allowing the negative mental states and negative moods to affect them. A master Hermetic, on the other hand, would do it consciously, unfailingly, and with a much higher degree of proficiency every time the negative swing threatened to ruffle their feathers.

The Master uses their will to attain a high level of mental firmness and poise seen as extraordinary in the average human being's eyes. The principle of polarity is connected to the principle of rhythm because the polarity demonstrates that rhythm exists between the two opposite poles. Hermetic Mental Alchemy essentially uses a combination of the principles of rhythm and polarity for countering and polarizing effect.

Most people can relate to the importance of the Law of Neutralization, thanks to their diminished ability to manage wildly swinging moods, feelings, and thoughts that threaten (and often succeed) to make their lives chaotic and intolerably difficult. Stop for a moment and recall how often a period of enthusiasm and joy was dampened by the power of an opposite feeling and mood.

You can think of the number of times when a moment of courage was shot down by fear and uncertainty. Tides of feelings rise and fall in most people. So, imagine if you had the power to hold the courage while being unaffected by the fear or to hold the enthusiasm and joy while being able to escape from the negative effects of depressing moods and feelings. That is exactly what the Law of Neutralization will help you with.

The Law of Patterns

The Law of Patterns is vital for human beings as they learn and understand the world around them by studying their environment's patterns. In fact, studying and understanding patterns has been a key survival technique for hunter-gatherer ancestors who lived at the mercy of nature.

Any good or bad habit or pattern tends to reassert itself over time unless you do something different and break the pattern. If you enjoy doing something and get positive feedback from your brain, you reinforce the pattern or habit in your mind. If you want to get rid of old inhibiting or "bad" patterns, you can use the power of spontaneous action by using new ways to do old things. This approach restructures and alters your thoughts, behaviors, and the way you live your life.

If you understand your internal patterns, it will help you see the dysfunctional habits you have. Changing the way you do things allows you to break these habits and restructure them, setting the course for an improved way of living.

It is not difficult to harness the power and significance of rhythm in your life. By harnessing the rhythm of your life and all things in and around it, you can be a conscious creator of your life path. Every time your rhythm is broken, learn to rise above it and set up a new rhythm to discover the unknown inside you. It is not easy to do this and will be fraught with difficulties. You have to learn to make a habit of discovering the unknown with you so that you can move ahead in the evolutionary process.

Your ego resonates at a low vibrational level. When you rise above your ego's vibration, you choose not to participate in the pendulum swing to the negative pole. This way, you become the creator and navigator of your destiny and life path. You get back the control of your free will to build self-awareness and recognize self-limiting and inhibiting patterns and habits. Once you identify these patterns, you can create conscious changes in your physical world whose effects will reflect your mental and spiritual world.

The Law of Compensation

The Law of Compensation states that the intensity of a swing in one direction decides the intensity of the swing in the opposite direction. You can see this law clearly in the physical plane in the swinging of a pendulum of a clock. The pendulum swings to one side and then swings equally to the other side. A pendulum with a short swing to the left will also have a short swing to the right. An object thrown upward to a certain height will fall back to the same height on its return journey. The same thing can be said for seasons, tides, and all phenomena of rhythm.

The physical manifestation of this law is obvious in all the scenarios explained above. However, the ancient Hermetics took this law a step further and said that a human being's mental vibrations are also subject to the Law of Compensation. This means that an individual who has a lot of happiness also has a lot of sadness. Someone who does not feel pain too much can also not feel happy to the same extent. All feelings and emotions are compensated for.

The same goes for animals. Many animals enjoy keenly, but their nervous system and temperament are designed so that they suffer high degrees of pain. Some people have low degree temperaments wherein both their joys and pains are experienced at low intensities. Some people have high degree temperaments, which means that they could be ecstatic when the occasion arises and can be downright depressed on the other extreme. The rule for this is that every individual's capacity for pleasure and pain is balanced—the Law of Compensation in action.

There is another interesting hermetic corollary for this law of compensation concerning experiencing pain and pleasure. A swing to a high degree of pleasure does mean a swing to the same degree of pain. However, the negative aspect comes first, according to

Hermeticism. If you feel a high degree of pleasure, it does not mean you have to be prepared for an equal degree of pain or be ready "to pay for it." On the contrary, the pleasure swing is preceded by the correspondingly equal pain swing either in this current or previous life.

However, a hermetic master can supersede and escape the swing of pain by using the Law of Neutralization. The master raises themselves to the higher plane, thus escaping much of the effects of the pain swing felt in the lower plane.

The Law of Compensation plays a very vital part in human life. You will notice that everyone "pays the price" for what they have or do not have. So, if you have something, you lack another. Your friend or colleague might have something you lack but lack something you have. That is why everything in this cosmos is balanced.

No one can really eat their cake and have it too. Everything has its good (or pleasant) and bad (or unpleasant) sides. What you gain is paid for by what you lose, and this is true for everyone and everything in the world and universe. The wealthy might have the riches that the poor lack. However, the poor could have something that the wealthy cannot buy with all their money.

For example, a rich man might be able to buy the best foods and eat in the most luxurious dining places. But he might lack the appetite for the food or could have severe digestive problems, and envies the poor man who enjoys a simple, plain dish with relish and has a healthy digestive system.

This kind of balance works in all aspects of life, and the Law of Compensation can be seen operating everywhere, balancing and counterbalancing, and always succeeding in bringing the Pendulum Swing to the other side, even if the time taken is longer than usual, sometimes more than one birth.

Applications of the Principle of Reality

Before going into the applications, it might make sense to answer the question, "Why is there rhythm in this cosmos?" Hermetics believe that life's regular rhythm is essential to grow and develop and rise to the higher planes of consciousness as you imbibe and embrace the expressions as you move from one side to another, from one feeling to another, from one experience to another.

Repeated rhythms and repeated experiences in life are essential for you to know, as all the possible outcomes of the various, complex algorithms are part of the Infinite Being of which everything in this cosmos is a part of. Cycles, repetitions, and rhythms are essential for learning and experience.

When one nation rises and falls, you learn something from this cycle. You implement some of the lessons learned in the next nation, and as it rises and falls, you learn new lessons that could be very or slightly different from the lessons from the rise and fall of the earlier nation or civilization. And each time a rise and fall happens, your learning gets better. Hermetics go further and say that even the Infinite Being learns from individual experiences, thanks to the rhythmic repetitiveness of everything in the cosmos.

The cosmos and all its elements have laws to stick to. For example, tides flow out and in, and this flow has to repeat. So, you cannot find a tide that flows out and in, vanishes, and then comes back randomly, flows in and out for a while, and vanishes again. This is not what happens. The tides simply stick to the rules and flow out and in repeatedly, rhythmically.

So, now, how can you apply this principle of rhythm in your daily life? One way is by releasing resistance. Now that you know that all things occur rhythmically and a fall is followed or preceded by a rise, happiness by sadness, ecstasy by depression, and so forth, it would be futile to resist the rhythmic occurrences in our life.

When you choose to work from a place of acceptance instead of from a place of resistance or continuously saying no to things happening to you, you can work better with your reality to manifest your desires better. Resistance is a negative emotion and works against the alignment of your personality. Acceptance is a positive emotion and can be used to manifest your desires and goals better.

The next step to using the principle of rhythm effectively is to become aware of your internal mental, emotional, and physical rhythms and the external rhythms that impact you, your experiences, and your life. When you build awareness about these rhythms in your life, you can use the power of the rhythms instead of being used by them. You get to be in control when you know and can expect what will happen next in any particular rhythm.

Here is an example to demonstrate the effectiveness of being aware of the rhythms in your body. Suppose you have noticed that you feel more lethargic than usual on particular days in a month, and on another set of days, you feel energetic. Once you know this rhythmic pattern in your life, you can preempt those days and choose to use the energetic days to do physical work while using the less energetic days to do a light reading or something that does not need too much energy.

Taking this approach means you are not resisting the rhythms. Instead, your awareness and acceptance empower you to harness the energy in the rhythmic patterns to get optimal outcomes for yourself. In this way, you can amend your life to align it with the natural rhythms and cycles.

To reiterate, it would be futile and unproductive if you choose to resist and fight against the rhythms of the cosmos. Instead, it makes more sense to accept and embrace the rhythms and use them effectively in your life and attract happiness and joy for yourself and your loved ones. Rhythms are good because they allow you to preempt things and events, thereby giving you the time to brace yourself for the troughs or prepare to optimally harness the crests of the rhythmic waves in your life.

Chapter 8: Principle #6: Cause and Effect

The sixth hermetic principle, called the Principle of Cause and Effect or the Principle of Causation, as explained in the Kybalion, goes as follows, "*The cosmos runs on cause and effect. Every cause has its effect, and every effect has its cause. The concept of chance or a random act is merely an unrecognized law. There are multiple planes of causation. No one can ever escape the law of cause and event.*"

Everything that you see and experience is a result of cause and effect. The sixth hermetic principle states that nothing in this cosmos happens by chance and that all the effects you feel or experience today have been caused by an earlier experience and its related elements.

"Chance" is only a word that describes effects and experiences related to obscure and unknown causes. When you cannot decipher or see the causes of certain events, you call such events "chance" happenings. Now you will look at the etymology of the word "chance."

It comes from an old French word, "cheance," meaning "to fall or befall," which is related to the "fall of dice." Therefore, the word chance came to mean anything that happens randomly and unrelated to any cause. However, the truth is far from this misconception. If examined closely, the fall of the dice is not a matter of chance at all. Each time a dice is rolled and a certain number appears, it will follow the universe's infallible laws.

At the back of the dice, falling is the cause of a series of chains of causes that go back way beyond the reach of the human mind and imagination. The position, amount of energy the thrower uses, condition of the table, and many other factors form the dice's cause and effect, which is the number displayed. Moreover, there are unseen preceding causes that influence what turns out when the dice is thrown.

A good analogy to explain unseen causes is this. Every person can go back multiple generations, and their ancestors would be something like:

- Two parents
- Four grandparents
- Eight great-grandparents
- Sixteen great-great-grandparents

If you were to calculate forty generations, you could run into many million ancestors. So many of them had to happen for you to be born. The same holds good for any phenomenon, even a trifling event like a speck of soot getting in your eye.

It is beyond the comprehension of an average human mind to trace that soot to the early period of world history—back to when it was part of a tree, which, and, after millions of years, got converted into coal that was mined, refined, and sold to someone who would use it in a way that a speck of it would get stuck in your eye. But everything in this world can be traced back to its origins.

Therefore, nothing comes from nothing. You see this in all common, everyday aspects of your life. Here are some irrefutable examples of everyday occurrences of the cause and effect principle:

A farmer must sow the seed of the crop they want to harvest later on. They cannot expect to sow barley seeds and get wheat out of them. Nowhere in the world can or will a farmer expect a crop different from what they have sown. "As you sow, so you reap" is nothing but the principle of cause and effect.

It is strange to look upon a farmer who expects to harvest barley after sowing wheat as being unreasonable, but when it comes to your life, behaviors, and attitudes, you choose to turn a blind eye to this all-important hermetic principle.

You forget or ignore the common folk proverb, "What goes around comes around." When you are in a bad mood, you treat everything and everyone rudely and gruffly. However, you get angry when others treat you badly when they are in a bad mood. People do not realize that the anger and rudeness they show to others is coming back to them.

When you cannot find or recognize the cause of any effect—often driven by the fear of what you see in yourself—if you dig deeper, you tend to use excuses such as coincidence or chance for that event or experience. You do not want to find deep, perhaps disturbing, answers to the "whys" that often crop up in your life. Many people even use God as an excuse for it.

On the contrary, Hermeticism uses the principle of cause and effect and says that if you cannot recognize the cause of an effect, it is only because it's unknown to you; since, according to Hermeticism, nothing and no one can escape the principle of cause and effect.

Most people experience the effects of their desires, will, and agendas of people they consider stronger than themselves. For example, the cause and effect principle can be seen in various human life elements, such as political leaders, the government, the social environment you come from, your family, etc. Most people live their lives being moved around like pawns instead of playing the game of life on their terms. The principle of cause and effect states that it is possible to rise above others' effects and live consciously and thoughtfully.

A classic example of cause and effect can be seen in the philosophy of Karma described in Hinduism and Buddhism. According to these Eastern religious philosophies, Karma is action, work, or executed deed and the intent behind these actions. Karma is the result of such a deed or action. So, if a deed and the intent behind the deed are good, it will result in good karma. If the deed and/or the intent is bad, the result is bad karma. People carry forward their incomplete karmas across all lifetimes.

The Bible also talks about the principle of cause and effect. *"A man reaps what he sows"* is a classic, timeless adage reflecting the cause and effect principle. The Bible says that the person who gives in to the desires of his sinful nature will reap destruction, and the one who works to please God will reap eternal life.

An alchemist uses the principle of cause and effect to regain control of their life. A Master Hermetic can use this principle in conjunction with the principles of vibration and mentalism to conquer their qualities, feelings, personality traits, and moods to transform from being a pawn to being in control of their life.

An alchemist also sees the principle of cause and effect as an effective tool to overcome past traumas and their effects in the form of limiting thoughts and beliefs. This approach helps people act and live with improved awareness. Since everything in this world manifests through the cause and effect principle, the one who masters the principle can become a cause instead of the effect. The master can harness the sixth hermetic principle's power to manifest their heart's desire consciously.

The Principle of Cause and Effect in the Economy and Politics

Unfortunately, the important sixth hermetic principle is treated disdainfully, or worse still, ignored in economics and politics. Many political leaders, regardless of nation or political party, pretend to take responsibility without really caring for vital human virtues like honesty or the consequences of their policies and decisions on the population.

Thoughtless policy decisions such as the indiscriminate cutting down of trees in an abundant rainforest in the name of progress have had disastrous effects with the rapid depletion of greenery and forest areas on the planet. Most leaders turn a blind eye to the effects of such actions, especially the long-term and nearly irreversible effects on the climate, environment, and wildlife, all of which can result in disaster for a vast majority of common people in the long term.

The same goes for policies that allow factory farming, which is a cruel way to kill animals for food. Also, the meat from such factories is not healthy for consumers. Additionally, these factories release a lot of carbon dioxide, which enhances pollution in the environment. Such actions' unpleasant effects will be felt later by all human beings, while a few people tend to make a quick buck in the short-term horizon.

The effects are not limited to policymakers or governments either. All the naive and innocent people who consume such meats are participating in this cause-and-effect chain, which affects the health industry, where new diseases are cropping up, making healthcare costs rise and ruining people's health at the same time.

These are simple and easy-to-understand cause and effect chains in the field of economics and politics. As a common citizen of the world, you must be aware of these causes and effects and learn to make wise choices, at least in your personal life. As an increased number of people make wise choices, the effects of it will be felt in the industry, especially when the profits fall for the concerned companies, and they will be driven to wind up such policies and bring in better ones.

Bob Proctor, the famous author of best-selling self-help books, mentions an interesting episode in his book, *You Were Born Rich*, which describes how the law of cause and effect works impeccably. He describes a meeting of eight private individuals who together controlled more money and wealth than the United States government. They were meeting to discuss how they could influence the government's policies—that was the kind of power they wielded.

The author then goes on to discuss what happened to these eight powerful men after 35 years. In a nutshell, they all died infamously, with some going bankrupt, developing cancer, and being sentenced to life in prison. None of the eight had a peaceful end in their home, and that is the effect of the actions they took in their youth when they had access to power and money. In this way, everything and everyone is covered by the law of causation.

The problem with most people is that they do not see the bigger picture. Many don't have the vision to see things in their entirety. They either forget or ignore the cause when the effect hits them. The cause could go far back in the past. So, it is likely that they have forgotten it. In fact, often, when difficulties hit, people are not even conscious of the underlying causes. You must remind yourself that there is nothing like an averse or unkind fate. Everything is a rebound of your previous actions that become the cause of the effects.

In the cosmos, nothing gets lost. Everything is saved and recorded, and the effects start building up as soon as the cause is done. It works like a butterfly effect where the flap of a butterfly's wings can create an earthquake in Japan. This can also be compared to the snowball effect when a little snowball rolling down a hill can create a gigantic avalanche.

Now, look at the law of causation operating in everyday life. There is interesting teaching in Hermeticism, and it goes something like this, "*To gossip is worse than murder.*" If you must kill someone, you have a clear cause concerning why and how you will do it and know what consequences you have to bear. On the other hand, you have no clear intention or knowledge of consequences when you gossip about someone.

You have no idea how your words about someone might spread and how the rumor can expand and blow out of proportions into something entirely different from what you said. You would not even recognize when this totally altered rumor hits you again through the grapevine. You are likely to think this has nothing to do with your own "harmless" gossip.

There are so many cases wherein seemingly harmless gossip spread so badly that the affected person lost their job or their reputation was ruined, and in some extreme cases, it resulted in suicide. The individual who started the gossip would then have to bear the effects of the gossip, regardless of whether the person did it with the intention to harm or not.

However, neither the gossipmonger nor the eight men who died horrible deaths would realize the avalanche of effects they created by that seemingly simple act. In both situations, the concerned people would have likely believed that life had been unfair to them.

These examples and the principle of causation tell you that you have to be careful about what you bring into this world. You might forget or ignore what you did or said to others. However, the consequences of your actions will hit you, no matter what. Suppose a father treated his family, including his children and his wife, cruelly—forcing them to do his will with complete disregard for their needs. In that case, it could be that this action returns in the form of loneliness or an incurable, painful disease in his old age, and no one would care for him then.

This is only an illustration of one of the probable effects of the man's behavior. The universe has a host of options available to fulfill the principle of causation for such a person, and people, with their limited capacities, cannot even begin to understand the alternatives available in the wide cosmos.

The only thing you should remember is that each time you think of doing something wrong or doing anything to harm, you must stop, think, and remind yourself that the boomeranging effect of your actions will have the same intensity as the way you caused them. Therefore, wise Hermetics always avoid shortsighted actions and thoughtless words.

Using the Principle of Causality to Your Advantage

If you know, acknowledge, and embrace the principle of causality in your life, you can take conscious steps not to behave in ways that are likely to rebound on you with negative effects. For this law to work, try making the world a better place instead of harming it. All the good you do will return to you with the same intensity and certainty you exhibited while doing the good. The outcomes might come to you in surprisingly different ways than you anticipated. But the intensity and the certainty of the rebound will not fail.

The Law of Karma (an important tenet in Hinduism, Buddhism, etc.), which is the same as the principle of causation, is explained wonderfully by a famous Indian yogi called Swami Yogananda. One day, the yogi's brother wanted to see how the law of karma worked. So, the yogi decided to give him a live demonstration. Both decided to travel to another city by train. However, the yogi laid a condition that they should not carry any money, not even a penny, in their pockets.

So, they went to the railway station, stood on the platform, and waited for their train to arrive. A distinguished-looking man stood a little away from them and was watching the two men carefully. After a while, he approached them and asked if it was really Swami Yogananda in person. After receiving the confirmation, the stranger's face lit up with joy.

He told the swami that he had been waiting to meet him in person and requested the swami to accompany him to his city (the same one they wanted to travel to) and spend the day there. Of course, he would take care of all the expenses, including food, accommodation, and travel. The brother was stunned to speechlessness watching the events unfold. All this happened because the swami always lived in accordance with the law of karma, and this instance was a rebound of one of his numerous good actions.

Another important reason to live by the law of causation is that people vibrate at higher frequencies. Gossiping, hatred, revenge, jealousy, and other negative traits have a low vibration. Living per the law ensures that you do not meet such people, thereby saving a lot of time and energy that can be used for better purposes. Moreover, negativity causes much stress, which can be avoided when you live positively doing good actions.

Summarily, the principle of causation or the principle of cause and effect states that everything that happens in the world has a cause behind it. As enlightened people, individuals can choose not to be affected by a cause and instead choose to make their destiny. This law teaches one to be self-reliant and live the life they dream of instead of being carried away by others' opinions and ideas.

Also, by following this law, you become conscious not to do anything that could rebound on you and cause negative effects. You can teach yourself to do only good so that the good comes back to you because the principle of causality teaches that what goes around comes around and what you reap, you sow. So, you can reap good rewards by sowing good thoughts and actions.

Chapter 9: Principle #7: The Feminine and the Masculine

The Kybalion states that gender manifests in all planes of existence. Everything in this cosmos has feminine and masculine traits, characteristics, and principles. The principle of gender is the seventh and last principle of Hermeticism.

The word "gender" is rooted in the Latin word "genus," which translates to generate, procreate, beget, or produce. In Hermeticism, gender does NOT refer to the physical sex or the male or female reproductive parts of an individual. When sex is discussed in the normal routine language, it is the manifestation of the hermetic principle of gender on the physical plane, which consists of organic matter.

In the physical planes, everything, including plants and animals, is continuously reproducing by combining the male and female characteristics. Inside every organ and organism in the physical plane, cells continuously replicate and create new cells through the power of creative catalysts they receive when they need to produce. The physical plane's reproduction process consists of mixing and mingling male and female energies and characteristics to produce new life. The opposites come together to catalyze and create new life.

It is vital to know that everywhere, including the physical plane, genders are not pure. To illustrate, biologically speaking, every female has some masculine elements, and every male has some feminine elements. While in most cases, the manifestation of female elements in a man, and male elements in a woman, are subdued and not very prominent at the physical level, the combined existence of both elements in everyone is visible at the level of the mind or the way one thinks. At the mind level, all human beings use both masculine and feminine energies.

From the perspective of Hermeticism, it is important to eliminate limiting ways of looking at gender, which is only in the form of physical sex. In Kabbalistic teachings, when talking of masculine and feminine energies, it is about the manifestation in the mind and spirit. Masculine energies include reason, logic, analytical thought, drive, and will. Feminine energies are all about creativity, intuition, imagination, emotion, and empathy.

The difference is clear. In Hermeticism, masculine and feminine energies are not relegated only to sex and physical characteristics. Instead, the various aspects of gender are discussed, including the thought processes and how the minds work. Masculine energies are rooted in the left brain, whereas feminine energies are right-brained. Also, the left brain is considered masculine, and the right brain is feminine. Now, remember every human being has a left and right brain and, therefore, every person has masculine and feminine elements within their body and mind.

Masculine energies are analytical and objective, and in many ways, you can refer to them as straightforward, simple, and even cold. Feminine energies are more emotional and nurturing, which calls for being less analytically and more subjective, considering each person's emotional and nurturing needs are different. Therefore, feminine energies are more complex and less straightforward than masculine energies.

It is vital to know that Hermeticism does not say that all men are analytical, cold monsters with no capacity to be creative or nurturing or that women are all intuitive, passive beings with no capacity for drive or will. Every human being has a mix of these male and female energies.

Therefore, a man (biologically speaking) may have more feminine qualities, such as creativity and intuitiveness. So, this man could be more intuitive than analytical in his approach to anything and everything. He may lack the drive and the ability to plan things out logically. He could be a creative person focusing on creating new things and a nurturing outlook.

Similarly, a woman could have more drive and a highly analytical thinking process, which means she is likely to take an assertive, ambitious life approach. She could lack the nurturing and creative urge and would rather prefer to plan logically and analytically. This does not mean that she is a man inside or that the man is a lady inside. The concept of gender in Hermeticism is not about sexuality leanings at the physical level.

Gender talk in Kabbalistic teachings is about masculine and feminine energies everywhere in the cosmos and in our consciousness. According to the Kybalion, the feminine is about receiving impressions, whereas the masculine is about giving or expressing impressions.

When individuals can mix up these qualities in a balanced way, they can express themselves well and find the desire and drive to achieve what they want. You can spend a little time analyzing yourself and trying to see what aspects of the masculine and feminine energies dominate you. When you do this, you will know what needs to be done to bring about a healthy balance of the two so that you can achieve self-actualization.

On higher planes and in different realms, gender manifests itself in various ways. In Hermeticism, the idea of gender being seen everywhere allows you to see how both the masculine and feminine energies operate and work together to create all things in the three planes of existence, namely the spiritual, mental, and physical. The manifestation of the female and male energies can be seen in the following phenomena:

Atoms are created when the masculine and feminine energies of the electrons and protons combine.

The combination of positive and negative charges and vibrational energies produces a host of useful and productive phenomena such as heat, light, electricity, alteration, magnetism, chemical affinity and repulsion, and more.

In magnetism and electricity, the positive end or pole is the masculine, and the negative end is the feminine. Negative, according to Kabbalistic teachings, is not "negative" as in evil or bad. It is simply the pole opposite the positive, and for electricity to flow in a circuit, both positive and negative poles are mandatory. In a magnet, too, there would be no magnetic field if either the negative or positive pole was absent. Both need to come together to create a magnetic or electric field.

In hermeticism, masculine energies are described as assertive, penetrative, progressive, and continuously striving to move toward their feminine counterparts. Feminine energies are sacred, receptive, treasured, and protected. The feminine energy honors priority, maintains traditions, and nourishes the essential elements of life.

Even in the field of science, feminine aspects are critical. Einstein said, "It is more important to be imaginative than knowledgeable" because knowledge is what you have here and now, whereas imagination covers the entire world and cosmos and can embrace what is now and here as well as what went in the past and what will come in the future.

Therefore, even research scientists who depend on humongous amounts of data to do their work need feminine energies to connect with their intuition and feel the outcomes of experiments, methods, and surveys that they conduct analytically.

Feminine energies are all about receiving impressions and creating new thoughts and ideas by following intuition and feelings. Masculine energies are all about giving out and expressing, and this is usually done analytically. The masculine energy is associated with the will, and the feminine energy is described as the receiver of impressions from its masculine counterparts to generate and create new concepts, thoughts, and ideas.

The feminine energy restrains, reasons with, and orders the masculine energy, which would otherwise result in chaos. In the absence of its masculine counterpart, feminine energy would constantly reflect and think and not take any action resulting in complacency and stagnation.

Here is an example of how a balanced combination of male and female energies can help you achieve your best. Suppose you are a YouTuber, and you need to create effective, engaging videos for your audience. You would need to use a mixture of masculine and feminine energies to create videos that connect with your audience. You would need the feminine aspect of creativity to think of a good idea for your video.

You would have to delve deep into the female intuitive energy to feel the content to render it so your audience will enjoy it. Feminine energies of nurturing will help you get insights into what should be said and at what time. Other female energies you might use include emotion, love, and other feelings needed to make an effective video that connects with the audience.

However, if you do not use the masculine energy of drive, will, and ambition, you might not be able to sustain your channel for long. Every new milestone you create for yourself in building your channel's strength and audience would require drive, will, and ambition, all of which are masculine energies. Without these elements, your channel is likely to fizzle out after the initial novelty wears off. Also, the masculine energies associated with analytical thinking, logical planning, and determining how to move forward are vital for your channel to thrive.

So, you see that for anything to thrive and succeed in the long term, you must be able to access and harness both your masculine and feminine energies, regardless of whether you are a man, woman, or transgender. This example also demonstrates the hermetic interpretation of gender, which goes beyond physical discernment based on sexuality.

Therefore, the masculine and feminine energies are interdependent, and one needs the other to flourish and thrive. Thoughtful action of the feminine energy and the effective use of the masculine energy, will, and vision combine and work in conjunction to bring about manifestation. These ideas are also represented in Hinduism through the concept of Kundalini.

Kundalini is the feminine energy that lies dormant at the base of the spine of all human beings. It remains dormant until it connects with the masculine energy, which directs the feminine energy, also called shakti, toward the head or brain up the spinal cord. When the two meet at the crown chakra, there is a spiritual rebirth for the individual. The concept of female energy is seen in the Bible's Book of Proverbs, where Solomon talks about wisdom being a feminine force that has always been God since the beginning of time, helping Him create the universe.

The hermetic principle of gender is closely related to the principle of duality or polarity. In both these principles, two sides of a coin are discussed. In the gender principle, the two poles are masculine and feminine, and the aim is to bring these two extreme poles together in a balanced way to use both characteristics optimally. Balance does not necessarily translate to the middle. It could be a point or place where you are comfortable and want to lean on. This is because everyone balances differently and experiences reality differently. Therefore, the balance for you could be more feminine than masculine or the other way around.

Balancing masculine and feminine energies is also dependent on your profession or the work you do. Many jobs are heavily reliant on masculine energies, such as finance, banking, insurance, scientific work, data collection, and other areas where analytical and logical skills are needed more than creative and nurturing skills.

Professions that are more suited for feminine qualities than masculine are home decorator, painter, artist, singer, or any place where you need to think outside the box. Social work also relies more on female energies because of the nurturing and caring attitude it relates to. Interestingly, some professions like architecture might call for both masculine and feminine qualities in equal measure.

Therefore, you do not need to balance in the middle. You could lean one way or the other depending on your personality, needs, and requirements. The trick is knowing and acknowledging the presence and power of both types of energies and ensuring they are used effectively. That way, you can lead a fulfilling and meaningful life even as you attempt to become a Hermetic Master, which would mean you have transcended beyond human capabilities.

While your profession and personality play a big role in determining what side of the gender scale you lean toward generally, you must remember that you could feel excessively different on certain days for no explicable reason. For example, even if you usually lean toward the feminine energy, you could make detailed logical plans on certain days.

There could be days when their creative urges take over for someone else with a masculine type of personality. Such situations are normal, too, and there are no hard and fast rules for gender operation. As an individual, you can choose to be conscious of everything happening in your life and align yourself to nature's way.

According to the Kybalion, the feminine principle holds the key to creation, and the masculine energy directs itself and other elements needed for creation toward the feminine aspect. Both the energies provide the fuel needed for creation. The masculine aspect provides the fuel for the drive needed to kickstart the creation process, and the feminine aspect's fuel helps in facilitating the nurturing and care of all elements needed for the creation process. Therefore, it is better to say co-creation instead of creation.

Yet, society is built largely on masculine energy. This is not referring to gender inequality or wage differences because that is a different issue. Now, look through the lens of Hermeticism. You can see that today's society is primarily masculine energy-oriented because nearly everything is done using pure logic and/or analytical thought. There is little or almost no touch of feminine energy, such as using intuitive powers, emotions, and feelings.

For example, if you see how the education systems work in society, it is logical and analytical with little space for creativity and intuition. The same holds good for politics, science, and technology. Most of the systems lean far more toward the masculine energies, thereby losing out on the benefits of feminine energies. Therefore, it goes without saying that if people want their world in general, and their societies in particular, to balance out, they need to bring in and harness the feminine powers more than they are doing right now.

Understanding the principle of gender is the ultimate step for an alchemist in their self-mastery journey through self-exploration. The knowledge of this principle empowers alchemists to recognize their actions, moods, and emotions and balance their feminine and masculine energies. Through this balance of masculine and feminine energies, alchemists find the key to unlocking the full potential of their powers of manifestations.

When an alchemist applies the principle of gender to the other six hermetic principles, everything in this cosmos comes within their reach. Nothing is impossible for such an alchemist or hermetic because they remain in tune with all the laws of the universe, thereby empowering themselves to become the ultimate being of light that God or Creator or the All Mind intended them to be. Such an alchemist takes full responsibility for their actions and harnesses the Infinite cosmic power to make this world a more beautiful place.

Chapter 10: Transform Your Life Through the Hermetica

Now that you know a lot about Hermeticism and its seven ancient principles, it makes sense to see how you can harness their powers and use them to transform your life for the better. Knowing the seven principles as a theory is one thing, but implementing their wisdom in your life is quite another.

Moreover, you must remember that Hermeticism is esoteric, and you must dive deep into its waters before you can unravel its meaning and interpretations. Now, look at each principle and see how you can use it to transform your life.

Principle of Mentalism

The Law of Attraction is drawn from this ancient hermetic principle. Everything in the cosmos is mental, and so, nothing exists without a thought. All the manifestations are nothing but responses to thoughts of God or the All Mind. Matter as you see and experience it is said to be a densified or focused spirit. Spirit is just a higher and more fluid level of matter.

Everything in this universe was created from thought. Even the chair you sit on, or the book you read was initially nothing more than a thought brought into tangible existence. Hermeticism says that in the same way, the first thought brought about an atom. This continued until, eventually, the world came into being. So, mentalism is all about creating the thought first and then bringing that thought into manifestation.

Now, if the cosmos is mental, your thoughts have far more power than you might know. The interactions of these thoughts on the spiritual and physical planes positively or negatively influence you, depending on your thoughts' content and nature. The first step to begin using the principle of mentalism in your life is to become aware and conscious of your thoughts and thinking habits and how they create and manifest in your external life.

Being conscious of your thoughts will help you apply the remaining six hermetic principles better. Here is a simple meditation technique you can use to become aware of your thoughts.

Sit comfortably in a quiet, undisturbed place. Close your eyes and take a couple of deep breaths until your body and mind are fully relaxed. Now, focus on the thought that is in your mind right now. Just observe it. Watch the thought growing and then slowly disappearing from your mind. Do not react or respond to the thought. Simply watch it like you would watch a movie.

When this thought disappears from your head, focus on the next thought. Watch it closely until it reaches a peak and gradually disappears too. Like this, keep focusing on your thoughts. Look at them from above, with your thoughts being people walking about, far below you. As they disappear from view, they are out of your mind as well.

It is not going to be easy because your mind is always dealing with numerous thoughts together. Start this meditation technique for just five minutes. As you get comfortable with the exercise, you can increase it by five more minutes until you can sit for about thirty minutes. The more you practice, the better you will control your thoughts and shift them whenever you want.

The Principle of Correspondence

The second hermetic principle, called the principle of correspondence, builds on the first. The second shows various planes of existence, where patterns in these planes correspond to each other. What happens in one plane happens in the other planes.

What happens in the macrocosm happens in the microcosm too. Everything is connected, so you can learn about one plane by learning about any other plane. For example, if you want to know how you feel, you can check on your physical state. If you feel physically fine, your mental and spiritual states are also more or less good.

To apply this principle in your life, you must increase your self-awareness. The more you discover about yourself, the more you learn about the external world. The more you learn about your actions and behaviors, the more you learn about how they impact your life and the universe around you. The cosmos and humans are interconnected, and what happens to you affects the cosmos and vice versa. You cannot exist without the universe, and the universe cannot exist without you.

Self-awareness is a key element of the law of correspondence. Look at your life and see what connections you can find with the world around you. The more you know about yourself, the better you will find it to know how you can think and act in a way reflected in your external life.

One of the best ways to start and build self-awareness is by starting a journal. At the end of each day, write about your day. What went right? What went wrong? What were your predominant feelings? What were the thoughts behind those feelings? Did your feelings trigger your thoughts, or was it the other way around? Would you have done anything differently now that your experience is in the past?

As you keep writing about your experiences, you will see yourself focusing on your experiences as you have them because you know you need to reproduce them at the end of the day. This way, you record your life and compel yourself to engage with your life in a deeper way than before.

After writing for about a week, go back to the first day's entry and read it. Can you recall the sensations and feelings you described in your journal? Can you find a connection with your feelings to the events of that day? Were your thoughts aligned with your feelings? The more you do this, the more you will find connections between your internal and external world.

The Principle of Vibration

The Kybalion says everything is in a state of vibration. Nothing rests. Matter, spirit, and energy are all vibrating at different frequencies. Like a chair or a table, even seemingly static objects are all in motion—although the vibration is not felt or seen by you. The atoms are continuously vibrating at different speeds and frequencies. Your thoughts also vibrate at varying frequencies.

Using this principle, you can transform and transmute your thoughts so that they impact your life positively. Changing your thoughts is the first step to transforming your life because everything is mental according to the first principle. Yet, changing your thoughts requires you to draw deeply on the power of your will.

When you transform your thoughts from one vibration to another, you can raise your physical existence also to a higher level. The more you focus on a thought, the more your life tends to grow in that direction. Therefore, start by becoming aware of your thoughts. What are the thoughts that limit your life, and what are the ones that expand your life? Once you recognize the negative thoughts, work on transforming them into positive ones. Here are some tips you can use to change your thinking from negative to positive:

Smile More Often — Each time you realize that your thoughts are getting negative, smile to yourself. This smile can be like a pulley that pulls you away from negative thoughts to something positive. Moreover, a simple smile to yourself can change your mood more than you know. Fewer muscles are needed to smile than to frown, and this makes you feel lighter. So, smile as often as you can.

Surround Yourself with Positive People — Positive attracts positive, and negative attracts negative. If you feel sad, go and speak to a friend who will make you laugh, and you will see that the negativity has flown right out of the window. Identify and recognize negative people and avoid them as much as possible. In contrast, get closer to positive people.

Change the Tone of Your Thoughts — For example, if your thought is something like, *I am going to have a hard time adjusting to the new roomie*, change it to, *I will face a few challenges when the new roomie comes, but the person is likely to come with some new ideas and thoughts that will help me.*

Like this, make the effort to change your thoughts because, if you do, your vibrations change, which, in turn, will trigger the law of attraction, bringing more positivity into your life.

The Principle of Polarity

The principle of polarity states that everything is dual, and there are opposite poles in everything. Opposite poles are identical in nature and only differ in degrees. So, love and hate are the same because they are both feelings, and they differ only in degrees. Poles are merely extremes of the same thing.

For example, how does a water faucet work? You can turn it on or turn it off (the two poles). However, it is up to you whether you want to run cold water or hot water. So, you see the faucet's water flow is not changing—only the temperature of the water is changing. The same holds good for all opposites. When the opposites meet, they become one.

How can you apply this principle to transform your life? You can use it to transform your emotions. You change your hate to love, from dislike to like, and so forth. You can cultivate a habit of focusing on positive emotions and diminish the power of negative emotions. Now that you know that both are of the same nature, you can embrace the hate and then work toward converting it to love.

The Principle of Rhythm

Everything flows and vibrates rhythmically. What starts ends, and what ends starts. The pendulum swings back and forth, and the right swing measure is equal to the left swing measure. Therefore, rhythm compensates.

Applying this to your life means accepting that all good or bad times will not last forever. This attitude will keep you humble and grounded when going through a good phase (when most people tend to become arrogant) and help you endure difficult times. As you slowly realize this truth, you will have nothing to fear or feel arrogant about.

You learn to take each moment, treat the experience of that moment respectfully, and engage with and enjoy it without worry, fear, or any other limiting emotion. Giving up attachment to your results and outcomes is a surefire way of applying the principle of rhythm to your life in a practical way.

The Principle of Cause and Effect

The principle of cause and effect (or causation) teaches you that nothing happens by chance. Everything has a cause and every action, thought, and behavior will result in some effects. Laws govern the universe, and these laws apply to everything in your internal and external world.

Often, people do not recognize the cause of the effects they are experiencing, especially the painful ones. They tend to label such instances as "chance happenings." However, there is nothing that happens by chance because every effect has its cause, even if it is not recognized.

How can this principle be applied in your life? Knowing that every action of yours will have a rebound effect on you will drive you to watch how you act, behave, and do things. You feel compelled to be proactive instead of being reactive. You take steps that will help you create the life you want. Instead of waiting for good times to come, you can act right now to create good times. You can act right now to become what you want to be.

The Principle of Gender

All things in the cosmos have two energy genders, namely masculine and feminine. To reiterate a point made earlier, gender in hermeticism goes beyond physical sex or sexuality. Masculine energy is assertive, has drive, and is forceful. The feminine energy soothes, restores, nurtures, and creates. Everyone has a combination of male and female energies, and it has no connection to sex or sexuality. A woman can have predominantly masculine characteristics, and a man can have predominantly female characteristics, and it does not take anything away from their biological sex.

To apply this principle to your life, you must observe what characteristics predominantly define you. What comes easily to you? Are you more of an analytical thinker, or do you use your intuition more? Once you know your basic personality, you can connect it with your profession and see your match. In case of a mismatch, you can either change your profession or how you think and behave or work on the traits to align them to your needs.

Hermetic Principles of Meditation

Any form of meditation practice is like a sun lamp that offers nutrition to a growing plant. In the same way, your meditation practice nourishes and nurtures your body, mind, and spirit so that you can grow energetically and spiritually. Meditation helps unfold your hidden beauty, talents, and inner peace.

During meditation, you are like the astronomer who is adjusting their telescope to bring something into focus so that they can study it in detail. In the same way, when you meditate, you are bringing your focus onto an aspect of your life that you want to observe closely and make positive and transformative changes to.

What is the purpose of hermetic meditation? It is to seek harmony with yourself and the world around you (like other types of meditations) and use the seven principles of Hermeticism to create harmony in your routine, everyday life. With hermetic meditation, you can improve harmony in your professional and personal relationships by dealing with your emotions and all other aspects of your life. With every practice, you learn to overcome and rise above your lower vibrations and seek higher vibrations until you understand and imbibe the power of the All Mind.

Hermetic Meditation is based on Franz Bardon's (a famous hermetic master) approach to this ancient tradition. It is a universal training program that develops your mind, spirit, astral aspects, emotions, and physical body so that your entire essence is in harmony and equilibrium with the cosmos.

In addition to compulsory twice a day sessions, hermetic meditation routines include specific exercises that improve and develop your meditating skills and prowess. It starts with the simple exercise of focusing on your breath, followed by focusing on your thoughts (a simple exercise is given in the initial parts of this chapter), and then focusing on no thoughts, and so forth.

Each stage of the hermetic meditation program is treated as a scientific experiment, and outcomes and processes are measured and tracked. For example, you would need to write down how many thoughts you counted as you meditated for ten minutes. You will notice that during the initial days of your meditation practice, there will be many thoughts. However, with practice, the number of thoughts will decrease because your focus has improved. These types of tracking and measuring methods are excellent forms of encouragement.

Hermetic meditation helps the practitioner gain control of and harness the powers of the underlying forces that control them, thereby giving the individual freedom to live life according to their dreams. As you sit in the meditation posture, you learn to slowly control your mind until you reach a stage when your mind is empty of thoughts.

You train your physical body to become strong and flexible so that you can sit for a long time without moving and your posture in perfect alignment during the entire meditation session. Through such sessions, you learn to connect with the higher force and harmoniously embrace your environment and live a life of fulfillment.

Mental Transmutation

Transmuting your mind and the mental plane is highly beneficial in all aspects of your life. Hermeticism uses the power of the seven principles to teach practitioners how to transmute to higher vibrations mentally. Mental transmutation works like how water in liquid form transmutes into steam (with fire), its gaseous form, with a higher vibration than water. It is the same principle to be used for your mind.

You can transmute your mind from sad to happy, from feeling bad to feeling good, etc. The fire needed for mental transmutation is your perceptive powers. By changing your perception, you fire up your mind to transmute itself the way you desire. When you change your perception from separateness to the idea of Oneness, you will find the power to accept and embrace everything and everyone around you with open arms and without judging them.

Therefore, using the seven principles of Hermeticism in your life can be done in countless ways. It is up to you to discover yourself and then make an effort to move toward higher vibrations by understanding and implementing the seven hermetic principles' power in your life.

The more you practice the hermetic way of life, the more harmoniously you will live with nature and the world around you. When you connect with the All Mind or the Creator or God (you can call Him or It by any name), you will realize the power of the Infinite Being's manifestation within you, and once this stage is achieved, nothing can stop you from doing your best and reaching your full potential.

Life is out there calling for you to live it according to your dreams and desires. Take the support of Hermeticism and get going because you deserve the life you dream of.

Conclusion

Hermetic principles, Hermeticism, or Kabbalistic teachings have been passed on for centuries through word of mouth. While the accurate dates when this philosophy was discovered are uncertain, there can be little doubt on its antiquity, considering its principles, thoughts, and ideals can be found in all world religions, either obviously or hidden from the eyes of the average believer.

Even today, the rules of multiple secret societies and occult teachings are founded on the principles of Hermetics. Hermetic teachings are alive and kicking today, and thanks to the power of the Internet, they are available to an avid student at his or her fingertips. However, it is important to note that you must not look for publicity as a true seeker but only use the principles to improve yourself and the world around you.

There were many reasons why Kabbalistic teachings were kept secret. One obvious reason is that if these powerful teachings fell into the wrong hands, they can be misused. Another vital reason is that hermetic principles and ideas are like a master key for independence and self-reliance.

Powers-that-be with vested interest throughout the history of humankind have determined not to share this kind of knowledge, which has the potential to dent their powers. They feared that ruling over a self-determined and "difficult-to-manipulate" population would be troublesome and unproductive. They would rather rule over obedient people through the use of limiting social standards and futile laws.

It is time to overcome these limiting barriers of thought and live life according to your desires and needs. And Hermeticism shows you that path of life. So, go on, reread the book and pick up lessons that you can implement in your life right away, and find the illumination you seek.

Here's another book by Mari Silva that you might like

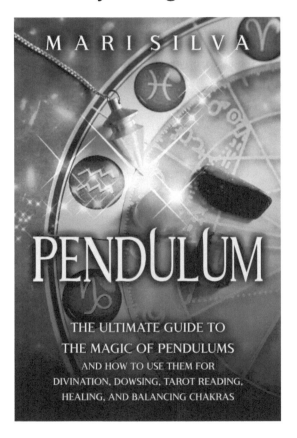

Your Free Gift (only available for a limited time)

Thanks for getting this book! If you want to learn more about various spirituality topics, then join Mari Silva's community and get a free guided meditation MP3 for awakening your third eye. This guided meditation mp3 is designed to open and strengthen ones third eye so you can experience a higher state of consciousness. Simply visit the link below the image to get started.

https://spiritualityspot.com/meditation

Bibliography

Alanna. "How to Use the 7 Hermetic Principles to Transform Your life." A Quiet Place. October 29, 2019. https://aquietplace.net/blogs/how-to-use-7-hermetic-principles-to-transform-your-life/

Ancient-Symbols.com. "Metal Symbolism." https://www.ancient-symbols.com/metal-symbolism.html

Ayam Journeys. Ayam Journeys: Self Empowerment Services. https://www.ayamjourneys.com/

Beyer, Catherine. "The Five Element Symbols of Fire, Water, Air, Earth, Spirit." Learn Religions. June 5, 2019. https://www.learnreligions.com/elemental-symbols-4122788

Crawford, Amy. "8 ways to raise your vibration (your positive energy)." Theholisticingredient.com. https://www.theholisticingredient.com/blogs/wholesome-living/13587702-8-ways-to-raise-your-vibration-your-positive-energy

Digitalis, Raven. "Magickal Influences and Principles of Hermeticism." Llewellyn Worldwide. July 12, 2019.

https://www.llewellyn.com/journal/article/2768

Evinity Publishing INC. Internet Sacred Text Archive. https://www.sacred-texts.com

Exploring your mind. "The Kybalion's Principle of Correspondence." January 9, 2019.

https://exploringyourmind.com/kybalion-principle-of-correspondence/

The Hermetic Nexus. "4 element vs. 5 element initiatory systems." October 23, 2011. https://hermeticnexus.wordpress.com/2011/10/23/4-element-vs-5-element-initiatory-systems/

Hierner, Sarah Sylvia. "The Foundation of All That Is: The 7 Hermetic Principles." Paracelsus-Magazin. August 15, 2019. https://www.paracelsus-magazin.ch/en/energetic-healing-methods/the-foundation-of-all-that-is-the-7-hermetic-principles/

Hurst, Katherine. "7 Hermetic Principles: Laws Of The Universe According To The Kybalion." The Law of Attraction by Greater Minds. March 18, 2019. https://www.thelawofattraction.com/hermetic-principles-kybalion/

jnolvx. "Harmony, Correspondences, and The Natural Order of the Elements." The Hermetic Herald. http://hermeticherald.com/2017/01/08/harmony-correspondences-and-the-natural-order-of-the-elements/

Kramer, Melody. "The Physics Behind Schrödinger's Cat Paradox." National Geographic. August 14, 2013. https://www.nationalgeographic.com/news/2013/8/130812-physics-schrodinger-erwin-google-doodle-cat-paradox-science/

Kuna, Natalia. "The Universal Principle of Mentalism." NATALIA KUNA | Psychic, Energy Healer | Spiritual Course Academy Launching 2021. http://www.nataliakuna.com/the-principle-of-mentalism.html

Mehrtens, Sue. "Jung and the Hermetic Law of Correspondence." Jungian Center for the Spiritual Sciences. January 29, 2014. https://jungiancenter.org/jung-and-the-hermetic-law-of-correspondence/

Mentalism Videos. "The Principle of MENTALISM Explained. No.1 of The 7 Hermetic Principles Of The Kybalion." https://mentalismvideos.com/the-principle-of-mentalism-explained-no-1-of-the-7-hermetic-principles-of-the-kybalion/

Merkur, Dan. "Stages of Ascension in Hermetic Rebirth." Esoteric.msu.edu. http://esoteric.msu.edu/Merkur.html

Mühren, Arno. "Introduction To Hermeticism — The Kybalion." Medium. December 4, 2019.

https://medium.com/@arnomuhren/introduction-to-hermeticism-the-kybalion-67d4ba6109f3

Robinson, Tanya. "An Introduction to Hermeticism." Falcon Books Publishing. January 1, 2017.

http://www.falconbookspublishing.com/what-is-hermetic-meditation/

Rogers, John. "What is The Kybalion." The Wealth Creation Mastermind. March 27, 2018.

https://wealthcreationmastermind.com/blog/the-kybalion/

Romain Noir. "The Principle Of Polarity." https://www.romainnoir.net/the-principle-of-polarity/

The Spaced-Out Scientist. "Hermeticism: the nexus between science, philosophy and spirit." June 1, 2015.

https://spacedoutscientist.com/2015/06/01/hermeticism-the-nexus-between-science-philosophy-and-spirit/

Three Initiates. *The Kybalion*. Martino Fine Books, 2016.

Wogan, Tim. "Do atoms going through a double slit 'know' if they are being observed?" Physics World. May 26, 2015. https://physicsworld.com/a/do-atoms-going-through-a-double-slit-know-if-they-are-being-observed/

The Wondering Alchemist. The wondering alchemist. https://www.thewonderingalchemist.com

Www.corax.com. The weird world of the Big Old Raven. https://www.corax.com/

Made in United States
Troutdale, OR
10/11/2023

13616001R00066